Praise for *Paren
*Grace and T

"Parenting isn't for the faint of heart. Seaborn presents a fresh, honest, and helpful parenting book built on the sure foundation of grace and truth. It is anchored in the clear understanding that every kid needs someone in life who is crazy about them, especially when life can get a little rocky. *Parenting with Grace and Truth* is a gift to help raise godly, healthy kids in a balanced and loving home."

—Dr. Tim Clinton, American Association of Christian Counselors President, Co-host Dr. James Dobson's *Family Talk*

"I'm a husband and daddy of two little children. From the moment I met my wife, Dan Seaborn has been a mentor to me, supporting my own marriage. He loves me with grace, but he loves me enough to not leave me that way. Patterns I've set in my own family are because he speaks truth to me. What I love most about this book is that Dan applies unbelievably practical helps even with the seemingly little time and energy you feel like you have as a mom or dad. Let Dan's parenting experience speak into your life. He gets it."

—Joshua Straub, PhD, Marriage & Family Strategist, LifeWay Christian Resources, Author of *Safe House*

"Grace and truth, along with the capacity and spiritual maturity to rightly employ them, are what set apart Christian mothers and fathers. They allow us to become the eyes and ears, the hands and feet, and ultimately, the love of God, to our sons and daughters. There are many 'voices' in the world today when it comes to parenting. Dan Seaborn brings an uncompromising and biblical approach to the subject, and incorporates humor, wisdom, deep insight, and balance to one of the most challenging roles in life. *Parenting with Grace and Truth* offers practical help with callouts, sidebar illustrations, case studies, questions to consider, and the use of story to bring home the principles he shares. This book is a must-read, and every parent will discover him or herself in its pages."

—Dr. Eric T. Scalise, PhD, LPC, LMFT, President of LIV Enterprises & Consulting, LLC, former Vice President of the American Association of Christian Counselors and former Dept. Chair for Counseling Programs at Regent University

"Few books have challenged my thinking and captured my heart like this present work by Dan Seaborn. His transparency compels the reader to go beyond the shallow waters of *traditional* parenting and venture into the deep and unfamiliar seas where God awaits to teach about grace and truth."

—Rick Rigsby, PhD, Pastor, Motivational Speaker,
Author of *Lessons from a Third-Grade Dropout*

"It's time for a reality check: There is no perfect parent except God. Anyone struggling with the balancing act of life and raising kids needs grace and truth. Blending biblical principles with practical steps, Dan Seaborn shows parents the path for equipping Christ-centered children in today's culture. This book will not only affect your child's life; it will impact yours!"

—Pastor Miles McPherson, Senior Pastor,
The Rock Chuch, San Diego, CA

DAN SEABORN

Parenting with Grace AND Truth

Leading and Loving Your Kids Like Jesus

SHILOH RUN  PRESS

An Imprint of Barbour Publishing, Inc.

Published in association with the literary agency of Credo Communications, LLC, Grand Rapids, Michigan 49525, www.credocommunications.net.

Cover design: Faceout Studio, ww.faceoutstudio.com

Published by Shiloh Run Press, an imprint of Barbour Publishing, Inc., P.O. Box 719, Uhrichsville, Ohio 44683, www.shilohrunpress.com.

Our mission is to publish and distribute inspirational products offering exceptional value and biblical encouragement to the masses.

ecpa Member of the
Evangelical Christian
Publishers Association

Printed in the United States of America.

Contents

Acknowledgments

I am grateful to God that I have been allowed to experience pain in parenting. It has made me more like Jesus. I would not have made it through that pain, or anything in my life, without the support of my wife, Jane. She has been my dearest friend throughout all of my life. I am dedicating this book to her and her faithful love to me.

I also thank my children who have prayed and stood by me over all these years! Alan and Annaliese, Josh and Amy, Cristina and Jonathan. I especially want to thank my youngest daughter, Anna, for her willingness to talk about our story together. As I write this book she is growing in Christ, and we celebrate all God is teaching her. We pray her life will have a mighty impact for Christ.

Also, thank you to Sue Lewis for partnering with me in writing this book. I appreciate the effort you put into it to make it exceptional!

I am blessed,
Dan

Introduction

Jesus forever changed parenting! When He came on the scene more than two thousand years ago, He brought a fresh approach of balancing grace and truth. He took some tired and well-worn laws and added joy! He was the first to say, "Let the little children come to me" (Matthew 19:14). His invitation assigned a value to children, who had never before been acknowledged. This gives us hope as parents that we can raise our children with the freedom that comes from grace and the love that is derived from truth. Jesus recognized the wisdom of God. He understood that whether there were to be one billion or seven billion people on earth, they would need a standard for living together in love and harmony. Jesus showed us by His example how to love—not force—God's principles into someone's life. While He endorsed and supported God's truth, such as that embodied in the Ten Commandments, He administered it with a gentleness to which people were likely to respond positively. By following His example, we will find hope and a future for ourselves and for our children.

CHAPTER 1

The Truth about Developing Good Character in Your Children

Christians are called to emulate Christ's character. Therefore we are going to take a look at Jesus' life and how He loved and then learn how to practice that same philosophy in developing good character in our children. The first thing we should notice is that our parenting style has to move from being authority driven to love driven. Wouldn't you want to be compelled to action by love instead of authority? As a father of four children, I learned how to shift from an authoritarian-truth style of parenting to a godlier and more grace-filled approach without ever compromising the godly standards I believed in. I will share the ways in which this has worked for me—as well as some of the ways it has not. We will analyze together why it is more effective to parent with truth and grace than with truth alone. For me, this shift in approach took away the burden of parenting as an obligation and turned parenting into an opportunity. It moved me from being intrusive to being inclusive.

To understand Jesus' character, we have to look at the Word of God and see the ways in which Christ's character models truth and grace. Many parents today struggle to understand the delicate balance between the facts—*truth*—and the Christlike manner in which we can enforce those facts—*grace*. Most kids don't like the facts. If you spend your time reeling off fact after fact to your children, eventually they are going to stop listening. That broken-record approach has not proven successful in most situations. But if you learn how to parent the same way Jesus parents us on this earth, with a pivotal combination of truth and grace, the paradigm will shift and character will begin to emerge.

Our children develop character in their lives by emulating our behaviors and by responding to how we discipline or encourage their behavior. Developing good character in your children is not easy, but it can be done. The goal is to help your children establish character traits that will assist them in the process of maturing into strong, capable adults who can successfully manage their lives with Jesus Christ at the center. While there is no patented formula that will produce the character you desire for your children, you can start by instilling the character traits that represent the values you want your children to emulate—honesty, gratitude, forgiveness, respect, and generosity, to name a few.

Character is about how your children behave or, more specifically, about how they react or respond to situations. It is a personal code of conduct that develops as your children grow and mature. Instructing children to be honest and then expecting that outcome isn't enough. You have to show them. A child won't know how to treat people with respect until you have modeled this approach. No child will be naturally inclined to forgive, but a child can learn how to forgive by watching you. Before people live by the truth, they have to see the truth in action and recognize its value.

ARRIVING AT AGREEMENT

The first step in establishing character in children is for their parents to agree together about which values are important. This might include sitting down with your spouse on more than one occasion and mapping out a list of character traits that you jointly believe are essential to infusing positive moral fiber within your children's psyches. To begin this process, think about your own childhood and the traits that were or were not encouraged in you. What example did your parents give you? How did you learn to distinguish right from wrong?

The Word of God already provides a foundation for the kind of character we should all seek to develop. Even though adults still struggle with abiding by these commandments, if you begin to teach them while your children are young, they will have a much stronger likelihood of not straying from them.

TRUTH

Start children off on the way they should go,
and even when they are old they will not turn from it.
PROVERBS 22:6

While agreement on values may sound like a simple objective, you may find a significant contrast between what you and your spouse were taught in your respective childhoods. You might be surprised by the different ideas your spouse brings to the table. One parent may have come from a household in which generosity, respect, and gratitude were regularly exemplified, while the other may have been taught that little white lies are permissible, gratefulness is expressed for the most part on birthdays and holidays, and respect is optional, depending on the circumstance.

That first step toward agreeing on what is important to teach your children can be complicated, but with perseverance the goal can be reached. This list of values will be critical because it will be the baseline you use to educate your children over the next twenty years and beyond. Agreement is imperative; otherwise even the best attempts at training won't work. Truth will be compromised and grace misconstrued. The parent who doesn't agree that a particular value is important will overlook behaviors and won't fight for what is vital.

ESTABLISHING RULES TO DIE FOR

My wife, Jane, and I refer to our list of values as "rules to die for." We chose to call them that because we cherish these standards of excellence so highly that we would risk our lives to impart them. We went so far as to list them on a plaque that hangs on the wall just inside our front door. Anyone who comes into our house can clearly see what is important to us as a family—the truth we strive to live by.

In developing this list of "rules to die for" we did more than just sit down and discuss potential additions as a couple. We actually sought out and brainstormed with mentors or other adults who in our opinion were doing—or had done—a great job of raising their children. Why reinvent the wheel? During that time I was a youth pastor, so I was in a position to meet a lot of kids, as well as their parents. I observed these kids in an environment where their true character was displayed—without

Only positive attitudes

Respect yourself and others

Abide by the morals we establish

Attend a place where you can worship God

Put ups no put downs

their parents watching. When I interacted with a teen whose character I admired, I sought out his or her parents for advice. Jane and I would treat the couple to a meal and then just sit back and pick their brains about what they were doing to inspire such great character in their children. Then we began to incorporate those nuggets into our own family life. It isn't that we took verbatim everything they said to us and incorporated their practices as our own, but we took all of the information given to us by all the couples with whom we met and decided together which approaches fit the values we wanted our family to embrace.

You don't have to be a youth pastor to encounter kids who exemplify the character traits you admire. Seek out friends or family members and gather their ideas for possible rules to die for. Then enlist the help of those closest to their kids to reinforce or model those ideals. For single parents in particular, this process could be extremely beneficial, though

I would highly recommend this approach for all parents. This practice will help you avoid the extremes of being narrow-minded or what I will call "loose-minded"—which carries in my mind a connotation slightly different from "broad-minded." If you do find yourself solo parenting, this practice may also help to relieve the pressure of raising children alone. "It takes a village to raise a child" is true of children of single and married parents alike.

Each family's list of rules to die for will be unique. What might rise to the top in your household may not be as big a deal to someone else. For example, one family might allow their teens to watch PG-13-rated movies at a younger age than another, while still another might forbid them at any time. Regardless of what list of family values you end up with, the most important consideration is that you have developed them together and are mutually committed to standing behind them. Consistently presenting a united front to your children and not hedging on rules you have already labeled nonnegotiable is critical. Children will walk all over and manipulate parents who are inconsistent or who disagree with each other. For you as Christian parents, that unswerving united front should itself be one of your rules to die for!

STEPS TO DEVELOPING RULES TO DIE FOR
1. Identify a family or families you admire.
2. Write down two or three nuggets of wisdom they share.

3. With that information as a foundation,
create your own list of rules.

COMMUNICATE THE RULES

Your rules to die for are not meant to be kept a secret. Once you have agreed on and established truths that will build character in your children, they need to be communicated clearly and in age-appropriate language. The most obvious way to communicate your values is to speak them verbally to your children. Certainly you can be creative in the presentation, but find a setting where you will have few interruptions and you can have their undivided attention. You will also need to reiterate and reinforce your rules from time to time. These rules will, directly or indirectly, be the stuff of conversations with your children throughout your lifetimes, but your greatest opportunity for getting this message across to them will be while they are still young and living under your roof.

THE POWER OF GRACE

Now comes the tough part. Making a concerted effort to come up with the rules and enforcing them with grace will require unending work backed by extraordinary perseverance. As parents, you have to follow through on these rules consistently, no matter how exhausted or busy you are at the time of a challenge or infringement. Most parents do a great job of communicating their rules and enforcing discipline the first couple of weeks or months, but as time passes, resistance slowly creeps in and begins to weaken resolve. You may grow weary of continuously dealing with the same issues and find yourself starting to ignore or turn away when you see something that needs attention. It won't be long, in fact, before you start choosing golf or shopping over problem-solving. We've all done it from time to time. At this point, the whole system behind the "rules to die for" can begin to slowly unravel, like a ball of yarn rolling down a hill. You will need to put your foot down and stop the madness before it overtakes your life.

I am currently advising a gentleman—a really nice guy who is still unfortunately very disconnected when it comes to dealing with the realities of his family. Like most of us, he sometimes prefers to ignore things that are happening in his home because, frankly, the job can be overwhelming. Or maybe he simply doesn't know what to do. But disengagement won't solve anything; far from maintaining the status quo, this approach will likely make matters worse. I have had conversations with this individual about the importance of his accepting and understanding his role as family leader. Sometimes exercising that role entails applying truth and grace that can be tough to come by. Nevertheless, it is a vital part of parenting. He, like you and me, needs to accept full responsibility for that which is his responsibility, because his children are watching and learning from his example. So even though he may be tired or hesitant because he is unsure of how to proceed, he needs to make sure he stays engaged and continues to participate in these critical aspects of parenting.

"Come to me, all you who are weary
and burdened, and I will give you rest."
MATTHEW 11:28

PAYING THE PRICE

Instilling character in your child will take longer than a day or a week. It will take years of teaching, guiding, and demonstrating what is important. Traits like gratitude, honesty, generosity, forgiveness, respect, humility, loyalty, integrity, and kindness will be internalized and valued by your children only if you take the first step to ensure that they understand and embrace their importance. Once you have established your rules to die for and communicated them to your children, be ready to enforce them at all costs. If they weren't important, they wouldn't come with such a high price—the cost of raising responsible children.

The progression entails establishing what the expectations are, clearly communicating the standards to your children, modeling the behavior you want to see from them, and consistently enforcing the rules and doling out consequences upon violation.

As the parent, *you* are the primary enforcer wherever and whenever you find yourself with your kids. You can't relinquish or soften your role when you are in the presence of others or when you are preoccupied or exhausted or just don't feel like parenting. Integrity and consistency are key. If we establish rules "to die for" that have no real or dependable meaning, we have defeated the very purpose for which we created them.

As you consider all that is at stake, think about the Ten Commandments and God's purpose for them. These truths are standards for us to live by—God's "rules to die for"! They were designed both to develop character in us and to protect us from harm. God knew that because of our sinful nature, we would need His guidance to be written down in terms clear enough so as not to be open to interpretation. That is the view I urge you to take of your "house commandments." Your children need to understand that these standards have been identified, defined, and developed by you, not by the opinion of your children's friends or what their parents may think!

"You owe it to your children to teach them to make the right choices in life by serving as their example and their mentor, not their best friend."

When one parent chooses to relinquish responsibility and places the blame for decisions or enforcement of the rules on the other, your authority as a parenting unit is undermined. This is true even if the two of you are no longer married to each other. It is especially critical that stepparents are on board and in agreement, or the children will be nothing more than confused. No matter what the extenuating circumstances, or even your physical proximity as parents, operating as one parenting unit is key to developing character in your children.

For that reason, it is essential that neither Mom nor Dad caves in on important guidelines to try to curry the kids' favor. Stop worrying about whether your children like you and focus instead on setting up guidelines that will help them succeed in life. Put simply, this is your responsibility as parents. You owe it to your children to teach them to make the right choices in life by serving as their example and their mentor, not their best friend.

HONESTY—THE BEST POLICY

When one of our sons was in third grade, his mother and I had to deal with an honesty infraction through balancing truth and grace. Being honest at all times is a "rule to die for" in our home. If it is also a non-negotiable for your house-hold, you have probably pointed out to your kids numerous times: "You will get into more trouble for lying than you will for whatever the offense is you want to lie about." As a friend of mine expresses it, "If you lie, you won't get by."

This particular incident came to my attention as I was driving home from work. I had called my wife to see what she was doing and to tell her I was on my way home. She told me briefly about her day and then said, "Honey, when you get home, you have to deal with a pretty significant issue related to one of the kids." Right then my heart skipped a beat. I rolled my eyes and felt my blood pressure rising. I was hugely disappointed. I wanted to point my car in the direction of the golf course and ignore my responsibilities, because the last thing I wanted to do after a tiring day was deal with one of the kids. But because I wanted to instill character within my children, I asked her to fill me in on the rest of the story.

"By the time I got home and my son and I had gone into what we call the 'wobble' room—a place where there is a little give-and-take—I was prepared for a great conversation."

She proceeded to tell me that our son Josh had admitted to cheating on a test at school. After I hung up the phone, I found myself fuming. I remember thinking, *Boy, am I going to nail that kid when I get home. I can't believe he would do that sort of thing!* Right at that moment, a convicting realization forced its way into my internal monologue: when I was in the same grade, I also had cheated at school.

The rest of my drive home was consumed with a conversation I had with myself about how I would talk to my child, incorporating an admission that I had struggled with the same scenario at the same age and stage. How would I explain that although this was unacceptable behavior, I had done the same thing? By the time I got home and my son and I had gone into what we call the "wobble" room—a place where there is a little give-and-take—I was prepared for a great conversation.

My son, however, looked sheepish and miserable as he slouched against the wall with his head hung. When he looked up at me, I found myself staring into the saddest eyes I'd ever seen. He looked like one of those hound dogs whose face looks perpetually sullen. Although I immediately wanted to comfort him and allay his fears, I knew he needed to feel the discomfort and to associate it with his actions. He explained to me how the cheating had come about, and when he was done I paused for a moment and then said simply, "Son, when I was your age, I cheated, too!"

Incredulous, he responded, "Really, Dad, you *did*?"

This surprised—even shocked—him, but I think my sharing that truth with him helped to take the edge off our whole conversation. He didn't feel so alone, and I stood there as living evidence that people can successfully recover from their mistakes.

We proceeded to talk about how important it was that he never cheated again. To ensure that he wouldn't, I told him he needed to confess to his teacher what he had done.

The tension returned to our conversation. My son's voice rose in pitch and urgency as he objected. "Dad, no way! I can't do that. I can't tell him I lied."

I replied, "Yes, you can—and you will."

My goal, of course, was to build his character. If I had covered for him and agreed not to tell his teacher, what good would this capitulation have accomplished? If he were to have played out that watering down of the principle into his adult life, he might eventually have proceeded to cheating at work, stealing from his employer, and surrounding himself with friends who would have condoned his behavior.

I believe it was on the day in that little classroom when

my sheepish son had to confront his teacher and say, "I cheated," that my son internalized a valuable lesson. He understood how much his mother and I value honesty and that disobedience would always have consequences. Does that mean it was easy? No. Had *I* really felt like going to my teacher way back when? Of course not, but confession needed to happen for my son to grow and understand the importance of honesty.

Grace isn't about letting your kids off the hook when they have done something wrong; it is loving them through their mistakes and as they deal with the consequences.

GRACE

At this, those who heard began to go away one at a time, the older ones first, until only Jesus was left, with the woman still standing there. Jesus straightened up and asked her, "Woman, where are they? Has no one condemned you?" "No one, sir," she said. "Then neither do I condemn you," Jesus declared. "Go now and leave your life of sin."
JOHN 8:9–11

Jesus didn't condemn the woman caught in adultery, nor did He condone her behavior. He forgave her and warned her to sin no more. Jesus showed his love for her by instructing her not to continue in a life of adultery (see John 8:1–11). He loved her through her mistakes.

By being proactive in your approach and teaching your children lessons through discipline and by example, you will save yourself a lot of future heartache. If you want to grow a garden that will yield fruit and vegetables for your family to eat, you will have to invest a lot of time and work up front. You will have to prepare the ground, plant the seeds, water frequently, pull weeds, and generally nurture the plants until they are fully grown and ready for picking. The same can be said with regard to your children. You will have to devote a lot of time and effort up front when they are younger in order for them to emerge later on as fully developed adults.

Good, honest, hardheaded character is a function of the home. If the proper seed is sown there and properly nourished for a few years, it will not be easy for that plant to be uprooted.
GEORGE A. DORSEY

MODEL IT

Whether you are teaching your children to be grateful, honest, generous, kind, trustworthy, loyal, or all of the above, the process starts with you as the example. Children won't understand what kindness looks like unless they have witnessed it in their own home. If children never see their parents giving to a church, a charity, or their community, either with financial blessings or through the gift of their time, they won't know how to be generous. Children learn gratitude from watching their parents say "thank you" or observing them writing notes of appreciation when they have received gifts. That is the benefit of modeling for our children.

THE END RESULT

Where our children end up in life will not be the result of one major right or wrong decision, but of the cumulative effect of a lifetime of choices, positive or negative, both witnessed and made on their own. Getting them to understand at a young age how the choices they make early on in life will impact their future is probably more critical than anything else you can do as a parent. A child who struggles with issues doesn't do so in a vacuum. In fact, repeated yielding to temptation may be the result of the numerous times a child has already made poor choices.

Now that you have a plan, please understand that kids will never fully cooperate. They will probably challenge you on every rule you have formulated, but they will learn fast. Once you discipline them for inappropriate behavior, they understand pretty quickly that you are serious about what you have said. If you fail to follow through with consequences, they notice that, too. They will begin to pick away at the cracks they see in the foundation, until pretty soon the whole edifice crumbles and you have nothing to stand on.

Don't settle for taking the path of least resistance. Be proactive, firm, and above all else, the person you say you want your children to grow up to be.

WHO, WHAT, AND WHY

Keep in mind three basic considerations whenever you are talking to your child about anything, whether in a discipline or a praise situation. First, keep in mind who you are talking to. Each child has a unique personality and will respond to your constructive criticism or praise based on his or her personal makeup. Don't apply the same technique or use the same words with every child. Figure out what works best for each child and adapt your style of parenting to fit that child's needs. For example, some children are motivated to behave well if they know they will receive a reward for their positive behavior, as opposed to punishment if they respond negatively. Employ the distinctive language that resonates with each child to help him grow into the adult you want him to be.

The second point to consider is what you were like at that age. While you don't have to reveal all of the poor decisions you may have made as a young adult, you can share some of them if the disclosure would help your child recognize your ability to empathize with what he has done. He isn't likely to consider that you remember and can relate to what it feels like to be his age.

The third point is to remember why you are responding as you are. Whether you are disciplining your child, praising him, or modeling a desired behavior, remember that you are trying to help him develop good character and become a productive citizen. You are working to instill within him positive character traits so that someday he will be capable of making his own appropriate decisions and will be equipped to treat others with dignity and respect and to function effectively and independently in society.

If you don't understand this as your ultimate goal in raising your children, you may end up with your adult children living with you for a long time. That usually isn't good for anybody. Enabling a child by capitulating to his every whim simply stunts his growth. With every word you say or decision you make, remember your overall purpose. This may not occur to you on a moment-by-moment basis, but the truth for Christian parents is that you are acting as you are not only for them, but also and ultimately for the glory of God. He is the One who has entrusted you with your precious children. A good principle to remember is this: by teaching truth with a covering of grace, whether or not your kids think this stinks sometimes, you are presenting yourself as a pleasing aroma to God.

TRUTH IN THE WORD

The Bible is one of the greatest teachers of character. Not only does it give us specific guidance from God on how to act, but the narrative portions are peopled with individuals who manifested plenty of character flaws but later emerged as examples for us to emulate. King David, the superhero of the Israelites, was an imperfect man who developed integrity through his many failures. Job, already identified by God as having excellent character, endured an inordinate amount of suffering. He rose to the challenge and further exemplified his integrity and faith. Jesus, who in his human nature faced more trials, challenges, and painful moments than anyone else in the history of humankind, provided us with the perfect example of how to maintain our character through the Word of God.

In Romans 5 the apostle Paul speaks specifically of Christian character. This chapter teaches us about the faith and peace that come through Jesus Christ alone. It teaches us that when we go through sufferings, the experience produces perseverance, and perseverance in its turn produces character, and character, hope—a hope that will not disappoint us (verses 3–5).

God uses the ups and downs we face as individuals and as families to develop our character and to implant within us hope in something beyond mere circumstances. Throughout this chapter I have talked about the importance of modeling behavior for our children. In Romans 5 we see why it is necessary for our children to see us go through trials and challenging times and become people of character and thus of hope. Our prayer must be that they will follow our example.

The Bible is the foundation for teaching our families. As parents, we may be tempted to teach our children lots of wonderful things without citing the Bible to back up whatever instruction we are offering. But when we omit this critical step, we fail to give our children everything available to us—and to them—to achieve success.

QUESTIONS TO CONSIDER

1. The "rules to die for" list is a tangible way to help establish character in your children by displaying truths to live by. Your kids will likely violate your rules at times. Remember that their disobedience is not a reflection of your parenting abilities but rather presents great opportunities for you to teach life lessons.

   What are your rules to die for? What are the consequences or outcomes of violating those rules?

2. Modeling behavior you want to see your children imitate is essential to building their character. However, sometimes you won't model the best behavior to your children. When that happens, point out your own less-than-perfect behavior, apologize for it, and move on. Modeling humility in such situations is vital.

   Is there a particular area in which you are not modeling consistently good behavioral traits? What can you do to change that?

3. Parenting is incredibly tiring, and you will have times when you will want to give up. The path of least resistance will be a very desirable option. Hopefully the tips in this chapter will encourage you to take a proactive stance more often.

   What tips from this chapter will you seek to implement immediately? How do you reenergize yourself when parenting makes you weary?

The following is a list of character traits you may consider implementing in your family. Remember to practice them yourself first—that in itself is the most effective teacher!

Traits to Consider

ambition	honesty	respect
commitment	humility	responsibility
courage	love	selflessness
dependability	loyalty	thankfulness
determination	obedience	
generosity	patience	

Here are a few practical ideas you can implement in your family life to ensure that the above traits are valued and practiced.

1. Focus on and teach one trait per week.
2. Tell a story to your children that demonstrates these traits.
3. Invent and introduce activities that highlight these characteristics.

For example, an activity to instill gratitude might be to have each member of the family acknowledge before a meal or bedtime something for which they are thankful that day. Consider doing this daily or weekly and not just at Thanksgiving.

To teach generosity, begin a practice of having your children give away their gently used toys when they are ready to upgrade or move on to something else.

Read books or rent movies that reflect whatever character trait you are trying to encourage. Be sure to engage in conversations with your family about these movies or books.

A child learns responsibility by being given responsibilities. Start when your child is young by giving him age-appropriate chores that will help him understand responsibility. Make sure to provide consequences if he fails to complete tasks.

To be effective, your ideas or activities don't have to be elaborate or expensive. Take some time to view the list above and jot down several ideas for how you can teach and practice these characteristics on a regular basis.

DAN'S REALITY CHECK

You may wonder whether incorporating all of these ideas will ensure that your children will grow up and make all the right decisions. I wish I could say that were true. The reality is that there are no guarantees, but there is hope that when you try to do the right things the percentage of successes will increase.

CHAPTER 2

Is Parenting with Grace and Truth Normal?

There is no such thing as normal in this world. What appears normal to one person is hardly normative for another. Still, we as parents continuously struggle with a desire for our parenting to fall within some elusive parameters that a majority—or some imagined panel of "experts"—might deem standard or appropriate. This idea originates at least in part from the continuous stream of feedback we receive from none other than our own children (hardly professionals in this area!) that nobody else's parents are doing things in quite the way we are! This barrage can be enough to drown our confidence! A variation is the standard claim that our child is the *only* child who doesn't get to do *that one* crucial thing. Do you ever wonder why "everybody else's" parents always seem to be saying yes while you are sticking with no? Is *that* normal?

Parenting can be a lonely job. And parenting with truth and grace can feel like solitary confinement because it seems that few parents care to utilize that model. But we can't afford to make parenting choices based on the decisions other parents make. The cost of failing is so high that this could be disastrous. Each child is uniquely created by the hand of God, an awe-inspiring, sobering reality that requires us to make thoughtful decisions that will benefit our own children individually, regardless of the apparent consensus of the larger body of parents. But what parent hasn't felt deficient, or at least deflated, when a child laments being the *only* one not getting to do something or go somewhere!

Parenting with truth and grace entails using Jesus as our

guide and standard. When we adapt the Jesus model, our actions will be based on a firm foundation, one that isn't prone to crumbling to the whims of culture. Even though our Lord sometimes allows circumstances into our lives that we don't particularly like or appreciate, we trust that He knows what we need better than anyone else—including us. A comparable dynamic exists between us and our children: we know what they need better than others do.

TRUTH

After I looked things over, I stood up and said to the nobles, the officials and the rest of the people, "Don't be afraid of them. Remember the Lord, who is great and awesome, and fight for your families, your sons and your daughters, your wives and your homes."
NEHEMIAH 4:14

UNDERSTANDING OUR NORMAL

You might wonder how you ended up parenting in precisely the way you do. How did your style evolve? You may not realize this, but everything we know, believe, and do is to some degree a reflection of the family we grew up in. Our beliefs about specific subjects and our approaches to various life choices—whether this involves a sports team we support, how often we attend church, whether we read books, or how we raise our children—all stem in one way or another from what we witnessed or heard in our household. This is how our "normal" was first established.

As you read that paragraph, you probably began to disagree—possibly even vehemently—citing in your mind specific areas in which you are acting in direct opposition to your parents' beliefs. Perhaps some areas in the parental approach you grew up with so rankled you that you have taken a deliberately opposite stance. That is exactly the point. The fact that you knew you were in opposition to your parents' views is proof that your view of normal began with your family.

As part of our Winning At Home organization, we run a counseling center. According to many counselors with whom I have spoken, issues related to family of origin are as common to counseling as adding and subtracting are to math. How people behave in any given area of life is the direct or indirect result of something from their childhood, adolescent, or teen years. Parents, or those acting in the role of parent or guardian, are the primary senders of messages directed toward children. Even if we don't behave in exactly the way our parents acted or prescribed for us, whatever we are doing is the result of a message they sent.

Interpreting those overt or subtle messages is a central part of everyone's story. Each of us deals with a different plot and characters, but the theme is the same in that we have all received messages from childhood that affect the way we parent. It doesn't matter whether our story reads like a fairy tale, a mystery, a Greek tragedy, or a thriller—eventually we will have to examine the chapters of our lives, understand how we filtered the messages we received, and learn how all of this ties into the parenting style we have adopted. Only then can we begin to close the book on the areas of our parenting style we dislike or feel are ineffective.

Feeling confident about our parenting ability is integral to our achieving success in this critical area. One confidence booster is feeling emotionally healthy about our choices. If we have never addressed emotional hurdles from the past, our insecurity will show in the way we parent. Just as the quarterback in a football game can't expect to complete passes with a broken arm, a parent who is suffering unresolved ill effects from the way she was parented can hardly expect to raise healthy children.

Being healthy is part of the way professional athletes and others succeed in their jobs, and the situation is no different when it comes to the job of parenting. The alarming truth is that our behavior as a parent is contagious for our children. Even the slightest exposure to unhealthy behavior can spread bad "germs," and soon enough our kids will be modeling whatever ineffective "normal" we may be exhibiting.

MODELING OUR NORMAL

Laura felt sick about the way she had yelled at her eight-year-old daughter, Maddie. She wasn't sure why she had done this, except that she had asked Maddie to put away her toys and had realized after ten minutes that nothing had been done. Her daughter was still plopped down in front of the television set watching her favorite show. Finding her there, Laura had immediately started haranguing her. She remembered Maddie's eyes getting big as tears started forming in the corners, soon spilling down her cheeks. But that hadn't made Laura stop. She had continued ranting until the phone had rung and she'd gone to answer it. While on the phone, Laura could hear Maddie crying and hiccupping in the next room. It had occurred to Laura that her daughter seemed almost afraid, even though it went without saying that Laura would never physically harm her daughter. Didn't Maddie know that?

Laura doesn't understand what comes over her in times like this. She somehow feels this is the only way she can discipline her daughter. After all, wasn't that the way she'd been disciplined as a child? Her mom would lash out verbally at the slightest provocation. Laura suddenly remembers how afraid she felt at Maddie's age. Laura really wants to be a good parent, but she isn't sure how to go about it. This is the only approach she knows.

Laura had learned from her mom that shrieking at someone is the only way to move them to action. To reestablish her normal, she needs to have a clear understanding of the issue at hand and deliberately choose a different filter to look through when it comes to managing behavior.

CHANGING THE FILTER OF OUR NORMAL

The reason you may need to change the filter of your normal, the lens through which you look at the world, is similar to the reason for changing your furnace filter. Its primary function is to protect the furnace by keeping a flow of clean air moving through it. The filter traps microscopic bugs, viruses, pollen, dust, and mites and prevents them from entering the furnace. If the filter isn't changed regularly, the air intake will be dirty, containing all types of contaminants—as will be the output of air. A clogged filter allows dust and other irritants to circulate in your home, negatively affecting the quality of the air you breathe. The more immediate concern, however, is that if the filter is never changed, the furnace could blow up and cause serious damage or harm to your family.

The same can be said about the emotional filter you may be looking through as you raise your children. If your decisions are based on a deficient model of parenting, your behavior may foster conflict with your spouse and ultimately damage your children. If you never change your filter, allowing ineffective behavior patterns to continue unchecked, over time it will clog up, at the risk of detonation. You won't be able to see clearly, and eventually this dysfunctional pattern will cause irreparable damage to your family.

MY DAD'S FILTER

I like to imagine those times when my dad and I sat across from each other at the dining room table and talked about life. Or played basketball together on

Saturday mornings. When I started becoming interested in girls, Dad was there to guide me through the maze of emotions and hormones. I found my faith through his leadership. I use the word *imagine* because, unfortunately, none of these things ever really happened.

In reality, I couldn't stand my dad for years. I didn't want to be around him. I didn't want him to ask me any questions. I didn't want any input or advice from him because I felt he wasn't there for me the way I thought a dad should be.

I scorned my father because in my view he sorely neglected my mom, my brother, and me. I am writing harsh words here, but I believe they are an accurate reflection of the troubled relationship we endured throughout my teen years.

Then something changed.

One evening, sitting at my parents' dinner table, I decided to take a risk based on a suggestion from my counselor. He had challenged me to ask my dad about his own childhood and teen years. Frankly, I had never cared about that because I was so focused on myself and who my dad was to me.

Dad opened up, and as I listened I could feel myself becoming emotional. He told me things that made my own kid-dom look pretty tame. He described scenarios he had faced as a teenager that helped me recognize his growth as a man. Understanding a little of what he had dealt with, I could tell he was trying to make a difference in my life.

In reality, my dad was even then struggling to change his child-raising filter. The situation still felt less than ideal to my brother and me, but discovering the truth about Dad's childhood helped me comprehend where some of his behaviors had originated. He was trying to be a better dad even though the result fell short of the image of the ideal dad I had created.

Just as changing your furnace filter doesn't typically call for the services of a professional heating and cooling person, this kind of reprogramming doesn't always require professional therapy. Once you are aware of the areas in which you feel deficient, you can set some goals and work toward changing your filter.

In Laura's case, one strategy might have been to count to ten before reacting to a situation of perceived disobedience from one of her children. Another tactic could have been walking away when she felt anger welling up inside. Or she might have talked to her spouse or a close friend before responding to the situation.

TRUTH

The best filter for us to look through is the one God provides through His Word. Interspersed throughout the Bible are various verses to which parents can look for their true filter. If you, like Laura, are parenting with a load of anger, one example might be Ephesians 4:29: "Do not let any unwholesome talk come out of your mouths, but only what is helpful for building others up according to their needs, that it may benefit those who listen." Realistically, no parent who reads this will always manage to keep from exploding at his child, but if parents sincerely want to assess whether their habitual reaction is the best possible response, they can find that truth in the Bible, for God is the perfect example of a Father.

HOW OUR NORMAL GETS STOLEN

When we initiate new behaviors, we might feel uncomfortable at first, as though we are walking around in a new pair of shoes we haven't yet broken in. We may feel pinched and hobbled and experience a bit of pain, but eventually we will hit our stride. Our new normal will eventually start to feel—well, normal!

The reason we worry about whether our parenting is normal is that we are habitually—and most often negatively—comparing ourselves to other parents. In reality, though, the only person we need to please is God. He is the One who has entrusted these children to our care, so it is His assessment that matters.

As a rule, when people compare they compare *up*. Our natural tendency is to evaluate ourselves against the standard of people we perceive to be performing better than we are. On the positive side, this decreases the likelihood of our self-evaluation breeding conceit. By comparing at all, however, we unwittingly allow those idealized others to rob us of the only normal that works for us.

Comparison is the thief of joy.
THEODORE ROOSEVELT

"Normal," as we have discussed, is the standard we establish for our family based on a variety of benchmarks, relating primarily to how we grew up, what we were exposed to, and how God formed our personality. So how is it we get sucked into fixating on someone else's normal?

The process starts innocently enough. As an example, consider an ordinary encounter with your neighbor. You start to chat about the weather and other insignificant things, and he slips in an observation about your landscaping. Not a compliment, but not necessarily an insult either. Your neighbor happens to spend hours meticulously sculpting his lawn and garden, while you typically spend your free time with your kids. You don't neglect your responsibility as a homeowner, but neither do you devote every waking hour to home maintenance. You feel it is more important to spend quality time with your kids, but somehow that niggling comment sticks in your mind as you evaluate your property. You tell yourself you don't really care what your neighbor thinks, but a tiny part of you does. You start questioning whether spending a lot of time with your kids instead of behind your lawn mower is normal. You had considered your norm to be appropriate and adequate until he made that comment. You are allowing your neighbor to steal your normal.

It is no different with parenting issues. You decide, based on your normal, that your teens' curfew will be 11:00 p.m.

Then you learn that a couple of their friends can stay out until midnight, and you start to question your decision. You are running the risk of letting other parents steal your normal.

Your son comes home from a friend's house and tells you about the new big-screen television they have. You look at your thirty-two-inch screen and wonder whether you ought to purchase a bigger set. Your concern about other people's possessions is stealing your normal.

Two of your daughter's friends are allowed to wear tops that expose their bellies, which have been pierced and adorned with various pieces of jewelry. Your daughter has been begging for permission to do the same, and you have consistently said no. But listening to her complaints, you wonder whether you just ought to give in. You start to feel as though your parenting is substandard or at least out of touch.

If you haven't established—or aren't sticking with—a normal with regard to your values in general, and your parenting in particular, you will continuously give in to the whims and desires of your children. They will keep challenging your decisions, asking you for stuff, or ignoring your requirements, and you will continue to give in to them based on what "everybody else" seems to perceive as normal. Society's apparent norm—whether or not your assessment of it is accurate—will become your normal, and you will look to television sitcoms, neighbors, and movies to help you decide how to raise your children. You will yield to cultural pressure instead of doing what you know to be best for your family.

Comparing your kids to others' kids can be equally as

dangerous, adversely affecting your perception of your child's normal. Every child is unique, blessed not only with a distinct personality but also with one-of-a-kind gifts and abilities. Comparing your child's report card with their friends' can be damaging for a number of reasons. First, you might expect your child to start doing better when she is already functioning at capacity. Alternatively, you might start feeling overconfident about your child's ability and transfer those feelings to the child, who in turn starts acting superior to her siblings or friends. Kids do enough comparing on their own. They are hit with a barrage of positive and negative comparisons in almost every interaction they encounter at school. Competition is a learned behavior, and parents need to be careful about making comparisons that might engender misconceptions and anxiety, jeopardizing their children's normal.

HOW NORMAL AFFECTS CONTROL

Now that we have figured out how our normal was established, we need to ensure that our kids don't steal it to the point that we lose control. As adults we need to maintain the upper hand in situations that arise with our children. For a variety of reasons, too many parents relinquish control to their children. Perhaps they feel guilty about a divorce, or their surrender might stem from their felt need to be liked by others, which may prompt them to give in to their children in the hope of being adored by them. Allowing factors like these to motivate the determination of consequences for disobedience can result in anarchy.

When we allow our children to steal our normal by

failing to discipline them, we eventually lose all influence with or authority over them. The goal is not for our children to be afraid of us, but a healthy respect on their part will help them understand that we can be counted on to follow through with the consequences we have established for disobedient behavior. For example, if our kids understand early on that we won't tolerate back talk, they will be less likely to engage in it when confronted with discipline they don't like. To be successful in that scenario, we have to set clear expectations for them to follow. They need to understand that if they participate in a certain kind of misbehavior, they will be punished accordingly. If we don't follow through with the stated consequences, we will begin to relinquish control; when that happens, we sacrifice our normal.

THE EARLIER THE BETTER

Your children have the ability to start stealing your normal from the day they are born. Skirmishes for control can start with minor situations when your kids are very young. For example, you tell your five-year-old son he can't have dessert if he doesn't finish his dinner. You put what you feel is an age-appropriate amount of food on his plate, and he proceeds to eat. He doesn't finish everything but still asks for dessert. You look at the half-eaten plate of food and say no. He starts to whine, complaining that he didn't like the taste of some of the food, but you stand your ground, reiterating the expectations you laid out before dinner. His eyes start to well up with tears, and his lips form a trembling pout. You can almost feel yourself starting to melt, and your resolve weakens. You start weighing the effort he made against your expectations and wonder whether your announced consequences may have been a little heavy for the situation. You start suspecting that he is a little tired or that you have given him an unrealistic portion. The crocodile tears start rolling down his cheeks, and before the first one hits his plate, you are setting a bowl of ice cream in front of him. Gone are the tears and pouty lips—as well as your control as the parent.

The scenario may seem insignificant at the time, but each time you give in to the whims of your children, they are systematically robbing you of your normal, and you are starting to lose both your authority and your ability to effectively parent. Start bracing yourself early on for the times when your children will be angry or upset with you. Their displeasure won't be terminal for them, but if you habitually give in to their desires based on fear of their response, you will gradually kill any prospect of respect from them. The key here is consistency. You need to follow through *every* time in *every* situation when you have set an expectation of consequences for disobedience. Persevering in the minor scuffles is key to eliminating more serious clashes later on.

TRUTH

No discipline seems pleasant at the time, but painful.
Later on, however, it produces a harvest of righteousness
and peace for those who have been trained by it.
HEBREWS 12:11

STICKING WITH YOUR NORMAL

The longer you let your children systematically whittle away at your normal, the longer it will take for you to regain control and begin operating once again within your normal. While wresting back control from a ten-year-old may take a while, this could take even longer with a sixteen- or seventeen-year-old—so much so that many parents succumb to the temptation to throw in the towel. That is why it is critical to establish your role as the parent from the start—based on your normal. Don't be swayed to change your mind or actions based on what someone else's parents may be doing—or not doing—or by what your kids may think. Your normal with regard to discipline is right for you and your child regardless of what anybody else is doing.

Diane's thirteen-year-old son, Jack, was invited to a friend's birthday party. After ice cream and cake, opening presents, and playing video games, the kids decided to go outside. With the permission of the birthday boy's mom, they were allowed to play "ding-dong ditch it"—with one stipulation: they were allowed to approach particular houses only if any one of the kids knew the homeowners. Along the way, the kids ran into some high school friends. After finding out what the younger boys were doing, the older ones suggested they try a particular house in the neighborhood, assuring the younger boys that the homeowners loved it when kids rang their doorbell and ran. Even though the younger boys were suspicious, they did it anyhow.

After several attempts with no answer, the kids were surprised when the police arrived. Although no charges were pressed, the officers wrote down the names of all the kids involved and sent them on their way. When Diane asked her son about the party, he said nothing about the incident.

A few days later, Diane received a phone call from the parent of another boy who had attended the party, and the whole episode was exposed. Diane proceeded to question Jack about the situation to verify the facts, and he confirmed that what she had been told was true. She disciplined him, though, for having omitted mention of the confrontation with the police. In her mind, that was the equivalent of lying. A few days later, her son complained that he was the only kid who had gotten in trouble over the incident. Some of the other parents, he reported, had even laughed about it.

Feeling uncertain about her disciplinary response, Diane phoned some of her friends to solicit opinions about what they would have done. Although many sided with her about her actions, some did not.

This is a classic case of a parent's normal being challenged, as well as an example of the importance of persevering through the small things. Although some parents might argue that the child had done nothing wrong, when Diane asked her son about the party, she was clearly looking for facts about what had gone on during the time he was there—the entire time. A visit from the police to a group of thirteen-year-old boys is worthy of mention to a parent.

GRACE

*Discipline your children, and they will give you peace;
they will bring you the delights you desire.*
PROVERBS 29:17

If Diane had done nothing, Jack probably would have felt more comfortable omitting facts the next time a problematic situation arose, or he might have chosen to outright lie. Ignoring the event would have been more convenient for Diane than going to the trouble of determining an appropriate punishment and listening to her son whine. If she had opted to ignore his behavior, however, her choice would at the very least have started a hairline crack in the foundation of her parental control—a crack that would have grown with each ensuing event for which she "should" have disciplined Jack but opted to avoid the hassle. Even the option of reversing the discipline after finding out that the other kids weren't being punished might have opened the door for Jack to begin challenging his parents whenever it came to consequences.

TRUTH

In this world we are faced with comparisons in nearly every area of life. Our beauty and physical shape are contrasted with Photoshopped pictures. We compare our homes to those pictured in reality TV shows. We are continuously encouraged to compare our spouses to characters in movies and books. And we compare our parenting skills with those of other parents in our own circles of acquaintances. Our normal—the way in which we have decided to parent—is continually being threatened by outside forces. In 1 Timothy 6:6 we learn that "godliness with contentment is great gain." It follows that we need to find contentment in the manner in which we have elected to parent. We have been given the standard of an absolutely perfect normal in the area of parenting. Our God, it goes without saying, is the flawless benchmark for us to use in all parenting situations.

QUESTIONS TO CONSIDER

1. All of your knowledge, beliefs, and actions on some level reflect your family of origin.

   How would you describe the way you were parented?

2. Being healthy is a factor in the job success of professional athletes and others, and the situation with regard to parenting is really no different. Your behavior as a parent— good or bad—is transmitted to your children. Even the slightest exposure of negative behavior can spread bad "germs," and soon your kids will be modeling whatever normal you exhibit.

   In light of the way you were parented, what are some learned behaviors you would like to change?

3. Once you become aware of areas in which you feel deficient, you can set some goals and work toward changing your filter.

   What simple steps can you take to change your filter?

4. You decide that your children's curfew is 11:00 p.m.—a decision based on your normal. But after you learn that a couple of their friends are allowed to stay out until midnight, you start to second-guess your decision.

   Who or what is stealing your normal?

5. We have been given the standard of an absolutely perfect normal in the area of parenting: God! He is the flawless benchmark for us to use in all parenting situations.

What scripture verse(s) can you find that back up your parenting behaviors?

_____

DAN'S REALITY CHECK

You probably won't stop making comparisons. This behavior has been a part of human nature ever since the serpent first stole Adam and Eve's normal. When Satan contrasted their limited knowledge against God's infinite comprehension, they suddenly felt deficient. Half our battle is becoming aware that we are comparing. So work on eliminating those comparisons whenever you can, and make a concerted effort to stop allowing people and things to rob you of your normal. Have faith in yourself as a parent, and put your trust in God to get you to that point and keep you there. God is flawless. He doesn't make mistakes. Your children are the very ones He intended for you to parent.

_____

CHAPTER 3

The Truth about Discovering Your Children's Unique Talents and Abilities

We worry about what a child will become tomorrow,
yet we forget that he is someone today.
STACIA TAUSCHER

All parents have dreams for their children. If you have ever been to a Little League game, you have probably witnessed a dad standing with his arms folded, bragging to another dad about the power of his son's right arm. Then they watch together as his son fires one across the plate. You just know that dad is envisioning his son one day pitching in the majors. Or perhaps you have been at a piano recital and watched a talented young girl run her fingers across the keys like a deer prancing through a meadow. You catch the twinkle in her parents' eyes as they imagine their daughter as the next prodigy. Or maybe you have watched the way a parent's face lights up when the teacher hands them a picture their child drew that day during class. You just know they are thinking their child could be the next Picasso.

In this chapter, we will explore the truth about discovering the unique traits and talents our children may possess. Some parents may fail to recognize them, or the picture may change because of unexpected circumstances. The initial plans we formulated in our minds (for our children to become pro athletes, president of the United States, movie stars, etc.) will eventually take a backseat to their own strategies; at some point they will become the drivers of their destinies, as opposed to going along for the ride.

It is possible, too, that the dreams and plans we have

forecast and broadcast for our children might ultimately limit them instead of expanding their possibilities. Sometimes we can get so wrapped up in our own ideas and hopes for our children's futures that we forget that an overriding plan, designed by God, is at play. That is why it is crucial for parents to pray for their children from the day they are born that they will move in the direction of God's will. God has a plan worked out for their lives, and your responsibility is to help them discover His direction. Helping them find their intended niches will require your patience and grace during these developing years. So even as you wonder about your children's futures, keep an open mind and wallet, bearing in mind that the plan that develops could be greater than the one you have envisioned.

TRUTH

In their hearts humans plan their course,
but the LORD establishes their steps.
PROVERBS 16:9

GROWING PAINS

As children transition from infants to toddlers to tweens to teens to young adults, they may be undecided about what they might like to do with their lives—beyond, of course, watching cartoons, playing electronic games, and exploring life online. There is, of course, the rare exception—the child who discovers his passion at an early age and grows up to be exactly what he forecast at the age of five. We as parents of the "regular" kids will expend a considerable amount of time and effort exposing them to a variety of activities, both academic and recreational, to help them figure out what they enjoy and identify their talents and abilities. Unfortunately, the progression doesn't necessarily follow in that order. Many kids discover what they enjoy, whether or not that matches up with or utilizes their gifts. For example, most young children like to sing. That doesn't mean, though, that every one of them should pursue this as a career, as most of us have experienced at one or another school talent show!

When children are preschool age, they have a good deal of free time. That makes it easier to involve them in diverse and multiple activities. Upon reaching elementary school, however, they will be assigned homework, and we will need to limit the number of extracurricular activities in which they can effectively participate.

Trying to figure out what our kids do or don't like—or are or aren't good at, or what can fit into their schedule without overwhelming them—can be a frustrating trial-and-error process. For example, what a six-year-old likes to do today may in no way resemble what he claims to enjoy tomorrow. And the day after tomorrow, he may throw a tantrum and refuse to participate. A slightly older child may resort to other avoidance tactics, like feigning illness or using homework as an excuse for not participating in an activity. On the other hand, children who end up loving an activity might become so absorbed they frequently "forget" to mention their homework.

Our parenting skills play a crucial role in deciding how to handle each scenario. What parameters do we set up to ensure that our children can enjoy their chosen activity while not neglecting other areas? Do we permit them to quit partway through an activity for which they have signed up because they decide they don't like it after all? How far do we push them when we see their reluctance to fully engage on the basis of shyness, lack of confidence, or even ineptitude that we would like to see them attempt to overcome? How do we say no when they really want to participate in some new activity but are already involved in too many others? One answer is doing the hokey pokey.

TRY THE HOKEY POKEY

You are at a wedding reception or other party, and several adults are standing uncomfortably in a circle on the dance floor, shifting from one leg to the other and glancing around rather furtively to see whether anyone else is watching them. Some are smiling nervously, while others are laughing and joking with the person next to them. A few people are being dragged into the circle. The kids are jumping up and down, unable to contain their excitement. The music begins, and a voice instructs people to put their right hand into the circle, remove it, and then put it back in and "shake it all about." The voice repeats, instructing participants to do the same with their left hand, followed, one at a time, by their right and left feet and then other body parts. Between the shaking of each body part, the group is instructed to do the "Hokey Pokey" and turn themselves around, concluding with a definitive chorus of "That's what it's all about!"

If you have ever attended such an event or have been to a roller-skating party with your kids, you are already familiar with the Hokey Pokey. I have tried to encourage my kids to play this kind of tentative, toe-in-the-water "game" in real life by putting their right arm into this or that activity—even if they withdraw it again quickly—or their left foot into some other variety of interest in an effort to discover what an activity is all about so they can determine which ones hold enough appeal to warrant more enthusiastic investment.

For example, my wife, Jane, and I thought all our children should take piano lessons. While they were small, feet dangling below the piano bench, squirming restlessly, they listened carefully to the clicks of the metronome while trying to stay in time with those first ditties like "Mary Had a Little Lamb." A couple of our children fell in love with music; the others wanted no part of it. By encouraging each to "do the Hokey Pokey," we figured that out.

The point is to allow your kids to try different activities without forcing them to continue with pursuits they don't enjoy. Don't assume that your child will delight in whatever it is that you as a parent are enthusiastic about. I have a son who, though he loves basketball, once told me that he felt I was pushing him in the sport. He went so far as to express, in so many words, his suspicion that I was trying to vicariously relive my own childhood through him. The truth can hurt.

At the same time, don't Hokey Pokey your kids to death. We have friends who allow their children to get involved in new things without letting go of old activities, thereby overloading their circuits. Sparks start to fly, and eventually the child's power source shuts down. Visualize, if you can, a person overdoing the Hokey Pokey. Not a pretty picture!

You are worried about seeing him spend his early years
in doing nothing. What! Is it nothing to be happy?
Nothing to skip, play, and run around all day long?
Never in his life will he be so busy again.
JEAN-JACQUES ROUSSEAU, *ÈMILE*

BURSTING AT THE SEAMS

I have talked to many parents who rue the fact that their kids are overscheduled. The dry-erase board that hangs on the kitchen wall to keep track of the family's activities has no more white space. The parents are well intentioned. They are striving to expose their children to as many different opportunities as possible to help them ferret out their unique propensities and gifts. The reality, though, is that there are many roads that will lead to your children's discovering their special niches. Extracurricular activities are just one way for a child to self-discover. It takes a lifetime for most people to realize their passions, and most of their searching happens after they leave home. If you think about your own journey and recall where you were at different stages of your own life, you can probably see the relevancy of that observation.

PARENTS WHO WEAR THE "WE'RE SO BUSY" BADGE WITH PRIDE

A vicious cycle has developed in the past couple of decades that has kids running around in circles. It is as though they are riding a Ferris wheel that never stops. Countless opportunities and options are available to kids today, and parents fear that if they don't let their kids try their hand at all of them they will miss out. This phenomenon even has a name! It is known as FOMO or Fear Of Missing Out, and as parents we all too easily get sucked into it. We plug in our kids here and there and everywhere until they become overstimulated and run down and start to disconnect. Their energy source becomes depleted, and they never get a chance to recharge their batteries.

We have moved so far in that direction that it is rare for families to spend unstructured time just being together—or for children to enjoy downtime simply enjoying their own "company." Both elements are essential for helping kids grow and mature. For example, recent studies have shown that families are unlikely to eat meals together on a regular basis because everybody's calendar is jam-packed. Parents seem to wear the "We're So Busy" badge with pride instead of with the more intuitive response of alarm or even disdain. And yet research indicates that children from families who eat meals together regularly, about five times a week, tend to achieve higher grade point averages[1] as well as have higher quality relationships with their parents.[2]

On the opposite end of the spectrum, studies have determined that this frenetic pace of childhood busyness is causing record degrees of anxiety. According to an article appearing on Time.com, the number of children with a diagnosable anxiety disorder has risen 25 percent, based on research conducted by the National Institute of Mental Health. The author describes some reasons for that increase:

> "Another way to think of anxiety is as a simple formula: Add up all the things that cause us stress, and then subtract all of our abilities to cope. The net result is our anxiety level. This formula makes it clear why childhood anxiety is on the rise. Schools are more competitive and stressful, children are more overscheduled, parents are worried about finances and safety, and our society is based on a win-lose model, where only a few children will be able to succeed. Meanwhile, coping mechanisms are disappearing: Children don't get enough time outside, either experiencing

nature or running around in their neighbor-
hoods. Children don't spend nearly enough
time doing "nothing," enjoying the downtime
necessary to process all their new experiences.
Instead, they are desperately engaged in a
drive to never be bored. I think many parents
have put themselves—and their children—
into an anxiety-producing corner. They want
their children to be academically successful
and always happy and creative and socially/
emotionally intelligent. It is an impossible
demand, and the inevitable result is anxiety
and burnout."[3]

That assessment is hard to argue with when we see this cycle
repeated all around us and within our own families. Spending time as a family is also important in helping children
identify their gifts. This setting offers a great opportunity to
sit down together and talk about what is happening in each
other's lives. Those conversations help our children learn who
they are and what they like, as well as understand how to
care about what other people are doing—stated another way,
this is about teaching our children to be in community.

"In community" is precisely the place Jesus wants us
to be. In Ephesians 4:2–4 Paul instructs his readers, "Be
completely humble and gentle; be patient, bearing with one
another in love. Make every effort to keep the unity of the
Spirit through the bond of peace." If we want to parent our

children like God acts in a parental way with us, we need to act more like Him, and that includes reading His Word so we can more fully understand His expectations for us. If our children discover their unique abilities but don't know how to interact with others, they may not be able to serve their God-given purposes. So enjoying family dinners together, or engaging in some other activity that is conducive to sharing, is part of training our kids in the art of conversing. Once they figure out who they are and what they want to do, they will be equipped to follow through in the company of others.

Parents have a tendency to focus on organized activities as the primary source for enabling their children to reach their potential in life. The reality is that this is only part of the equation—unfortunately, the part that can lead to overbooking our kids. The other impetus is parents' desire for their children to start building an impressive résumé that will get them into the best colleges and offer a shot at scholarship opportunities. The mad race begins already in elementary school, with the alarming result that children are becoming stressed out at very young ages. Too many essentially burn out before reaching college.

PUSHY PARENTS

In the very beginning, in those first moments of life, you hold your little bundle of joy, and when you look at him or her, it is as though an explosion of love detonates in your heart. You are instantly convinced that this tiny, wriggling somebody is nothing short of amazing and destined for greatness.

Overall, it is healthy to experience that kind of love for your child, and it is good for boys and girls to grow up knowing their parents believe in them. However, a love like this runs the risk of becoming distorted when we get pushy.

This dynamic can be observed at nearly every children's sporting event, elementary school play, or choir concert. If you look closely, you will find pushy parents everywhere—on the sidelines, in the bleachers—even in the wings backstage.

You can distinguish them from the other parents because their cheers are wilder and their frustrations voiced more vociferously, and because they typically complain when their kid isn't center stage. They grouse that the coach is lousy, the activity leader is blind, or whoever is in charge "just doesn't know talent."

Parents like this are never satisfied, even with their children's best efforts or achievements. There is always a note that could be truer, a skill that needs fine-tuning, an execution that somebody else does a touch better.

Forget about that once-amazing bundle of joy— no longer are these parents content with anything short of superstardom. It makes us wonder whether their children will ever experience the satisfaction of measuring up.

We as parents need to relax and let our kids be kids, to allow them to discover what they love and encourage them just to have fun with it. We may need to practice, but we can learn to make accomplishments and trophies secondary. We need to let our kids know we will always cheer for them, that no matter how objectively "good" they are at any given activity, in our eyes they will always be great.

Although most parents have the best of intentions when they choose extracurricular activities for their children, there are many other pathways by which children can discern their unique talents and gifts. Some of these pathways evolve from participating on teams and in other organized activities, but much experience can be derived from ordinary life as well.

When children engage in sports, the arts, or other such activities, they not only glean valuable technical skills but wisdom about life as well. Values like teamwork, dedication, hard work, service, and follow-through are revealed through organized activities, but these characteristics can also be learned through the normal course of a day. For example, completing homework assignments, tests, or simple chores at home help children understand the value of hard work and dedication while also learning to manage priorities. Daily activities with classmates or sharing with siblings can help children see the benefits of teamwork.

This is good news for the child who doesn't participate in myriad activities.

SOMETIMES KNOWING GOD'S WILL IS EASY AND SOMETIMES IT ISN'T

The question of what high schoolers will do with their lives gains urgency as SATs, ACTs, and decisions about college loom in the not-too-distant future. Some kids will be crystal clear about what they want to do, while others will vacillate. Some won't have a clue even up to freshman registration.

That was the case with our second son. There we were, three in a pack of hundreds of parents and kids crowded into a hallway waiting our turn to register for college. Several kids were lined up, cell phones glued to their ears or buds connected to their iPods, while they calmly awaited their turns. Others, like my son, were uncertain and insecure. We inched forward ever closer to our destination. By the time we reached our target, my son had settled on photography. At that point, to my knowledge, he had never taken a picture in his life except as a child when he had wanted to play with the camera and snapped a photo of his mom and me. Fortunately, by the end of his freshman year, he had a better picture of the direction of his life. God had made it clear that he should serve in some kind of ministry capacity, and he has since taken steps along that career path.

In contrast, our oldest son has known since he was about six years old that he wanted to be in ministry. I remember well the night he called me into his room. He was sitting up in bed, his eyes wide and misty, as he shared with me how God had spoken directly to him about the pastorate. I remember crying with him that night as I held him and breathed a prayer of blessing over his life. I have been amazed at how steadfast he has remained in his belief, even when others questioned his calling. At thirteen years of age, he asked for a transfer to a specific school where he would receive more Bible training, to which we readily complied. That son has completed his studies and is now engaged in full-time ministry.

Sometimes knowing God's will is easy and sometimes it isn't. The point, though, is not the degree of difficulty but whether our kids ultimately get to the place where they feel fulfilled and at peace. Keep praying for God's direction in helping your child find that niche!

HURT VS. HARM

Part of helping our children discover their unique talents and proclivities happens when we allow them to endure bumps and bruises as they navigate life. A parent's knowledge of when it is appropriate to apply first-aid treatment, as opposed to letting a wound heal on its own, is crucial to the process. Carefully thought-out decisions along this line build character, enabling our children to travel down the road of self-discovery. Allowing them to experience some emotional pain is critical, not only for distinguishing their strengths and weaknesses but ultimately for identifying their distinctive gifts.

A memorable illustration came for me when a friend described a couple of his son's middle school football coaches. During one of the first practices, these coaches talked to the kids about expectations involved with team membership. Since football is a heavy contact sport, they started out by explaining the difference between hurt and harm. Against that backdrop, they laid the ground rules of what would be acceptable during practices and games.

These coaches defined a hurt as something like a side ache, a bump, a bruise, or maybe a twisted but nonsprained arm or leg resulting from a tackle. These are not injuries that would require an ambulance ride or a stopped practice. They are a natural part of the game these coaches expected the players to endure and take in stride. Harm, on the other hand, describes injuries after which a player can no longer physically go on or might risk damaging his health by continuing. An injury might even require a player to stop playing all together.

The coaches did a great job of explaining the difference between the two concepts along with their ramifications. They understood the importance of pushing the kids a little under certain circumstances to increase their stamina and help them stretch their mental and physical limitations without going overboard.

Where parents do too much for their children,
the children will not do much for themselves.
ANONYMOUS

The expectations voiced by these coaches are similar to the kind we appropriately have for our children as they continue their discovery journeys. Parents who witness their kids experiencing hurts may need to push them a little to motivate them to stay in the game. This won't always be easy, but if we don't allow them to experience the natural consequences of their decisions or the negative aspects of an activity, they will be unable to fend for themselves when they get older. They won't discover their capabilities because they will be afraid to extend themselves, and they won't know how to live independently as adults. If we habitually step in and take over, they won't develop critical independent living skills.

Our kids will experience hurts of varying degrees nearly every day. Even if we wanted to, we couldn't attend to every physical or emotional scrape our children will experience. We will never even know about most of their hurts. But each time a child overcomes a hurt on his own, he will feel stronger and wiser for it. When our child is harmed, however, a different response is appropriate. Harm might result from circumstances like abuse, neglect, or bullying or other inappropriate behaviors on the parts of others. In football, harm may occur as often as once or twice a season; when it comes to our children's lives, we can only pray for never.

Exposing our children to various opportunities is a great

idea. But we are wise not to expose them and then leave them to negotiate the consequences on their own. Walk through those opportunities with them. Allow your kids to struggle or even to flop or fall. Just don't allow them to flop alone. Think of a fish lying on the dock, breathing heavily and wildly flailing in an effort to propel itself back into the water. Your child will need support at times. You might even have to pick him up off the ground.

Some of the best lessons a child and parent will learn come when a child is less than capable of completing a task. Such circumstances allow the child to feel hurt without enduring harm. Support him, affirm him, and care for him, but let the minor abrasions he experiences help to shape and toughen him. In the meantime, work with him to establish in his heart and mind who he is and where he is going.

THE GIFT OF ENCOURAGEMENT

The movie *Rudy*, which came out in 1993, is a true story of triumph and perseverance against difficult odds. Rudy was a young man who desperately wanted to play football for Notre Dame, but his grades were low, his athletic skills were deficient, and he was half the size of most of the other players. After two years at a junior college, he transferred to Notre Dame and secured a spot on the practice team. Within two years, Rudy exhibited more drive and desire than many of his big-name varsity teammates, earning the right to suit up and play in the last game of his college career. He ended up sacking the quarterback of the opposing team and was carried off the field by his teammates.

As a parent, I have learned that sometimes when my kids aren't as good as others, they actually learn some great life lessons *through* their deficits. Naturally, all parents want their kids to excel, but that desire can't always conform to life's hard realities. I remember talking to one of my boys about his disappointment at not being a starter for a game. Steering the conversation in another direction, I suggested that whenever my son was sitting on the bench, he could focus on applauding the talents of the players on the field. I went on to explain that as he did so he would develop his gift of encouragement. I loved watching my son clap and call out words of support from his place on the bench. By the end of that season, he was getting more playing time; I am convinced that had a direct connection to his attitude of celebrating others' abilities.

Nobody is going to be the best at everything. In fact, if someone advances to the top 20 percent in any given area, he is already far ahead of the majority in the field. We as parents therefore need to identify at least one gift we can celebrate with our child as he grows up in order to prepare him for the realities of life. The parents of above-average kids who become starters in middle school and high school need to be especially careful about preparing their children for life beyond that sport or activity.

No endeavor, even if it adds value and enjoyment to a child's life, should ever be allowed to *become* or define his life.

DISAPPEAR VS. INTERFERE

Nobody likes to see their kids experiencing sadness or dealing with hurt feelings. When children are young, we can easily divert their attention and soothe them by giving them ice cream, finding their favorite movie to watch, or simply changing the subject. As kids get older, though, the situation becomes a little more complicated. Well-meaning parents often try to run interference to prevent their children from getting hurt. Although they are acting out of love, parents who consistently interfere, attempting to solve problems *for* their children, may inadvertently sabotage the process of letting them grow and develop. If our kids are to truly understand and utilize their capabilities, they will need to accept that risks and benefits are intrinsic to the package.

If you want children to keep their feet on the ground,
put some responsibility on their shoulders.
ABIGAIL VAN BUREN

WORKING THROUGH HURTS

Dr. Peter Newhouse, director of the Winning At Home Wellness Center that provides counseling for individuals in our area, told me about a hurt his daughter experienced while playing volleyball on her high school junior varsity team. Though not necessarily the best player, she was above average, having made the team as a freshman. He shared with me some detail about one of her first games as a high school player. It was the last game of an all-day tournament, and the team was losing. He was sitting in the bleachers intently watching when, from across the gym, he observed the coach pulling his daughter from the game. She proceeded to yell at her on the sideline before temporarily benching her. The coach had been yelling at the team all day, as was her style, but her verbal barbs were particularly sharp during this game, most likely based on the frustration of losing. My friend couldn't make out exactly what the coach was saying, but his daughter's body language spoke clearly; her head was down and her shoulders slumped, and the bounce in her step had disappeared.

He doesn't think his daughter made any serious mistakes. She may have failed to communicate by shouting out whether or not she intended to hit the ball. As he drove her home, he asked her a few questions, but instead of answering with words, she burst into tears. She wasn't ready to talk, but clearly her feelings were hurt.

Later on, after she had showered and pulled herself together, she was willing to share more detail with him. After taking in the information, this father was confronted with several possible courses of action. The protective dad in him wanted to call up the coach and ream her out: What the heck she was thinking yelling at his daughter for what he considered an invalid reason? The counselor in him wanted to call the coach and ask whether she considered verbally bashing kids to be an effective leadership style. The judge in him wanted to get the other parents riled up about the coach's unfairness and then circulate a petition for her recall. The friend in him wanted to listen to his daughter and share with her some negative comments about the coach and her approach. One way or another, his response would be integral to whatever lesson his daughter would walk away with.

My friend understood that though his daughter had experienced a small hurt, she hadn't been harmed. If he had chosen any one of the more extreme options running through his head, he would have run interference with her, robbing her of an opportunity to learn and grow.

As each of us knows, there are two sides to every situation. Whether this coach's methods were right or effective was immaterial in the sense that his daughter needed to learn life skills like managing conflict, receiving criticism, and being challenged by authority. If abusive treatment had been happening, he would have stepped in immediately, but what had occurred with his daughter was a natural part of life. Not every coach yells, but every coach, teacher, boss, and coworker will influence our children in one way or another.

"If parents continuously rescue their children, they run the risk of sidelining or benching them from life, virtually cutting them off from critical real-life interaction."

As our children maneuver through dealing with the various personalities in their lives, they will learn valuable skills. These relationship experiences will be instrumental in the development of their own style, in the discovery of their abilities, and in reaching their potential in whatever they decide to do in life. If parents continuously rescue their children, they run the risk of sidelining or benching them from life, virtually cutting them off from critical real-life interaction.

Another possible response for a parent is to disappear from a situation or avoid dealing with it altogether, usually out of fear that he doesn't know the appropriate thing to say. An example might be a situation in which a dad and daughter are together and the daughter dissolves into tears. Some dads would lean in the direction of wanting to comfort their daughter or to beat up the person who had dared to hurt their precious little girl. But beyond such a physical response, they may fear that they lack appropriate helping skills.

Other parents disappear because they lack the time, energy, or inclination to deal with situations. But more often I find that parents, feeling inadequate, react passively by opting not to respond actively. A habitual lack of overt parental response can unfortunately cause children to develop into adults who try to take control of everything or have difficulty accepting help from others. Such children are forced to grow up independently because their parents have been unable or unwilling to effectively reach out when they have felt hurt or harmed.

Children have more need of models than critics.
CAROLYN COATES

From my perspective, the ideal role for parents is to observe from the sidelines and support, affirm, and care for their children whenever possible without intervening. Parents are wise to coach and guide their children, while limiting their interference to avoid short-circuiting the learning process. When our children have been hurt or disappointed, we can simply offer to listen, or we can acknowledge our awareness of what has happened and feel their sorrow with them. We might opt to share the memory of a time when we experienced the same kind of hurt. We don't have to be professional counselors to show them we care.

SUCCESS VS. FAILURE

When we consider success and failure in terms of our children, our first thoughts jump to what they can or cannot do; we naturally lean in the direction of performance-based concerns. But overall success in life is a far more critical matter, and parents play an important role in helping their children develop a view of success that ties in with how they will ferret out the puzzle of their giftedness.

The manner in which we define success in our own lives is most likely based on perspectives our parents instilled in us as we were growing up. This might not have involved specific words but was based on what was valued, both inside and outside our homes. No one family can excel in every activity, meaning that each family eventually settles on a few areas on which to focus their time, effort, and money.

DEFINING SUCCESS

Success is defined in any given family not so much by what we say as by what we cherish. If we treasure the tenets of our faith, positive moral and religious values, and education, these will be key components in our children's view of success. It isn't that we talk about them every day, but we do regularly attend church, behave in a manner we want our kids to emulate, and make certain they attend school and work diligently to the best of their ability. It is largely through that nonverbal, modeled exposure that our children will come to understand these as areas our family values along the path to success.

God defines success by how well we manage—by how well we steward, to use another model—what He has given us. God already knows our strengths and weaknesses. He created us, after all, and deliberately equipped us with them. And He encourages us to grapple with these issues to be successful with what He has given, commensurate with the level of ability in any given area with which He has endowed us. We aren't all meant to perform the same task in the same way. God created diversity because He needs many different skills to accomplish His purposes. This is the bottom-line reality for all of us who put our faith in Jesus Christ. Are we accomplishing His purposes and bringing glory to Him by effectively managing the abilities He has entrusted to us? Stepping back, do we even *know* what our gifts and abilities are?

Consider the parable of the talents Jesus told in Matthew 25:14–30. A man is going on a long journey and leaves some of his talents, or money, with each of three servants, entrusting each to invest the money according to his level of ability. He leaves five talents with one servant, two with another, and a single talent with yet another. Upon his return, the master discovers that the first servant has doubled his currency, allowing him to return not five but ten talents to the master. The second has also doubled the amount. Both are told that because they have done a great job, they will be trusted with still more. The last servant informs his master that he has kept his talent safe; and having done nothing with the trust, he dutifully returns exactly what he was given. The master, disappointed, directs this nonproductive servant to give his single talent to the man who has doubled his investment on the initial five talents.

God has gifted each of His children in such a way that our gifts perfectly complement those of others. He doesn't simply tell us one day what our gifts are, opting instead to help us expose them through our own efforts. It is our responsibility as parents to guide our children's self-discovery. As you help your children develop their strengths and detect their unique talents, bear in mind that God doesn't intend for them to be successful by the world's standards but to use their gifts to bring glory to Him.

There are only two lasting bequests we can hope to give our children. One of these is roots, the other, wings.
HODDING CARTER

I am not suggesting that the specific areas I have cited should constitute the ideal focus or value system for all families; worthy as they are, I mention them only as examples to illustrate that although you may not be speaking overtly about your definition of success, your actions speak volumes to your kids. Notice the families in your neighborhood or social circle. You may observe a family in which Grandpa was a pastor and members of the next generations have followed suit, opting to become involved in some type of ministry or service position because they grew up learning that a significant facet of success lies in serving others. Along a similar vein, we all are aware of notable families, numerous members of whom have involved themselves in civil service positions such as the military or politics. Those people grew up regularly attending military functions or volunteering for political campaigns. They have naturally come to define success as involvement in some aspect of public service.

Consider both the statements and the reinforcing actions you are communicating to your children on a regular basis. One of your neighbors gets a beautiful new car, which one of your kids mentions in passing at the dinner table. If you respond just once with "Yes, it is very nice," your kids probably won't think twice about the exchange. But if you make five or six comments about the car throughout the evening and again the next day, you are communicating to your children that you view a new car as a sign of success.

Another scenario might involve a dad and son who attend events together on a regular basis. Dad habitually makes comments about nice-looking women who walk by. What message is he sending to that young man? Dad is, perhaps inadvertently, communicating that the physical attributes of a woman define her beauty. Similarly, if both parents work fifty to sixty hours a week, don't carve out special time for family, and spend all of their free time with cell phones pressed against their ears, they are by their actions defining success as working without a thought for maintaining balance in life.

On the positive side, if your kids repeatedly observe you buying stuff the neighborhood kids are peddling door-to-door, giving at church without hesitation, donating your decent used clothing to local charities, and expecting them to set aside a portion of their allowance for charity, you are defining success, at least in part, as the ability to be generous. If you regularly say please and thank you to whomever is serving you, remember to leave a room exactly as you found it, and are courteous to everyone with whom you come in contact, your children will understand that politeness is critical to success.

We might define success in the same way as our own parents, or we may have a completely different set of ideals. Between those two extremes, we may communicate many of the same values as our parents, possibly with a few additions or changes.

Your children's degrees of success in life won't be solely dependent on what they can physically accomplish; rather, their success will be based on the condition of their hearts, on who they are as persons. All of the activities with which they become involved are part of the clay that God in His good grace will use to shape them into the people He wants them to be.

TRUTH IN THE WORD

We all are born with distinctive gifts, each bequeathed to us by the God who alone can view the bigger picture of the body of Christ. He has distributed all of His good gifts in a way that allows the body to work together as a functional unit. As Paul puts it in Romans 12:6–8, "We have different gifts, according to the grace given to each of us. If your gift is prophesying, then prophesy in accordance with your faith; if it is serving, then serve; if it is teaching, then teach; if it is to encourage, then give encouragement; if it is giving, then give generously; if it is to lead, do it diligently; if it is to show mercy, do it cheerfully."

Our focus as parents shouldn't be primarily on whether our children have the gift of playing basketball or the flute or performing in some other way; instead, we are called to look for and recognize the spiritual gifts that God has seen fit to give them. It is even possible that we will discover along with our children their spiritual gifts during the course of their participation in various activities. It isn't wrong to want our kids to pursue excellence in the activities they enjoy, but if we don't encourage their use of their unique spiritual gifts, we will be encouraging them to pursue excellence in the wrong place. This is confirmed in Hebrews 2:4: "God also testified to [so great a salvation] by signs, wonders and various miracles, and by gifts of the Holy Spirit distributed according to his will."

As you think about helping your children uncover their unique gifts and talents, don't get so caught up in the things of this world that you fail to recognize those special gifts given by God and manifested through the Holy Spirit.

_____

QUESTIONS TO CONSIDER

1. All parents dream about their children's futures.

    When you dream about your child's future, on what do you tend to focus? Could your dreams somehow be placing limits on your child's potential?

2. Children can be fickle. The activities they like will vary from year to year and, for younger children, even from hour to hour.

    How do you handle situations in which your child excels in an activity but doesn't want to follow through with the initial commitment, especially if there is a financial outlay for participation?

3. Many children today are overscheduled—bursting at the seams with their commitment overload. Their parents feel compelled to prevent them from missing a possible opportunity that could help them in the future. The result is a vacant dinner table or tightly scheduled, hurried mealtimes.

    How do you ensure that your family has time together and that your kids' lives are well balanced?

4. Some parents push their children to the brink in terms of their achievement expectations. Even when these

expectations exceed the children's ability, the parents continue to look for more.

How can you avoid being a pushy parent and opt instead for contentment with your child's performance level?

5. It is impossible for us to protect our children from the hurt that will occur in their lives. Some hurt, in fact, is necessary if they are to grow into mature adults.

    In what areas of your children's lives do you tend to be over-protective? In what situations have you felt a need to push your children?

6. Your child's view of success may be due in large part to what was practiced and communicated in your home on a regular basis.

    How do you think your child would define success if you were to ask him? Consider doing just that to see what he actually says.

DAN'S REALITY CHECK

You may wonder whether involving your kids in a plethora of activities is hurting or even harming them. In reality, what one child can handle may be quite different from the tolerance level of another. How much is too much remains your decision. Evaluate each child according to his personality and make adjustments as needed, bearing in mind the gifts God has given him.

CHAPTER 4

The Truth about Parenting through a Crisis

When God designed creation, His plan was flawless and complete, with nothing left to chance. He included a man, Adam, who was to rule over the earth, and fashioned various creatures, each of which was brought before Adam to be named. Determining that Adam needed a helper of his own kind, God proceeded to create a woman, Eve, from Adam's rib. God's desire in creating humans was that they would multiply and eventually fill the earth. All of the resulting people would have fellowship with God and be blessed by Him.

In the beginning, when God looked through His view-finder, He saw a picture of a man and woman enjoying life on the planet with Him in the bodies He had given them. God's original plan was not for man to die but for him to enjoy everlasting life with Himself.

But something happened. When Adam and Eve disobeyed, sin entered the world and God's plan was changed forever. Because God is omniscient, He wasn't surprised by their actions, and He had a plan in place—a plan from which we still benefit today. The picture is different from the one God originally viewed, but He was able to adapt the negative elements for our good and for His glory. If we want to parent as God does, we need to learn how to accomplish the same goal.

A NEW PICTURE

Many of us are amateur photographers. We snap photos at family functions, on vacation, and in other situations when we want to capture a memorable time. Digital photography and camera phones have made this activity even more prevalent and simple. Think about the last photograph you took, which, considering today's culture, was likely recent. Did the picture in the viewfinder match up precisely with the resulting snapshot you viewed digitally on your screen? It probably didn't—perhaps prompting you to try again. You began by rearranging the objects and/or people in the shot, or by altering the location or lighting, to improve your chances for success. It is quite possible you ended up preferring the second result.

When we first gaze into the viewfinder of a newborn child's life, we see a picture of near perfection, an imprint of our hopes and expectations for what will happen for this newly minted little one. Unfortunately, the end result isn't necessarily what we anticipated. Children don't always make good choices, and parents don't consistently discipline or respond as they should. Possibly, as a result, a crisis may occur, causing the picture to be changed, sometimes irrevocably.

The unknown aspect isn't as much *if* your family will face a crisis as it is a matter of *when*. Each family is certain to come across a set of circumstances that will to one degree or another turn their world inside out and upside down. Any given family's definition of a crisis will be different. The situation may involve a long-term or chronic illness, a tragic accident, or even the death of a family member—examples of the kinds of unforeseen crises that can be said to happen *to* us, generally not as a result of poor choices any of us has made. On the other hand, there could be a criminal offense or an issue related to internal violence—upheavals with a behavioral or choice component, the kinds of crises on which we will focus here. No matter what the particulars, when families are faced with life-changing circumstances, they tend to categorize the event as either good or bad, in much the same way they evaluate photographs. Understandably, they tend to dwell on that aspect, as opposed to recognizing the event as something that, though neither hoped for nor expected, has nevertheless occurred. The picture hasn't turned out the way they may have wanted, but they retain the option of re-arranging the shot and can strive to embrace the new picture as much as they did the original.

Consider the example of a child who becomes addicted to drugs or alcohol. While we know this is not a good situation for any child, we as parents need to try not to focus solely on how bad the situation is, disabling us from actively moving from there into resolution mode. The same applies if our teenage daughter becomes pregnant. Naturally, we as parents would be upset about this situation and might even be concerned about our reputation in the community, but getting stuck there won't help. Parents tend to respond according to one extreme or the other: they either beat themselves up over the crisis, fixating on how they could and should have prevented it, or they go into apathy mode, effectively washing their hands of any responsibility. A third and complicating scenario might be that one parent lays the blame on the other. Nothing good can come from any of those reactions; there needs to be a delicate balance between the excesses. I am not suggesting that parents don't need some time to get used to an idea or situation, but as a rule it is healthier to move beyond negativity and find productive ways to deal with the issues—to figure out a way to adjust the picture.

TAKING RESPONSIBILITY

The first step in navigating a crisis is to take realistic responsibility for whatever role we as the parent may have played in the event. This entails getting in the right frame of mind and figuring out our role in coming alongside our child and walking with her through the situation. This is a process in which the whole family needs to engage, and therefore it will take time. It can't be accomplished by simply flipping an emotional switch. Recognize that everyone's time frame will be different in terms of when she or he reaches that point of acceptance.

_____

"Great families can hopefully grow closer and become more united in the face of tragedy."

_____

Whatever the tragedy, our response as parents is the factor within our control. For all family members to get through the crisis, everyone will need to take some responsibility. If, on the other hand, people fixate on blaming and shaming, it will be difficult for anyone to move forward.

For us as parents, I believe there comes a point at which we need to evaluate the steps that may have led to the crisis. We need to look as objectively as possible at factors like discipline and decide whether the methods we have used with our child have been effective. Were there sufficient boundaries in our child's life, such as appropriate curfew times? Did we get to know our children's friends and/or their parents well enough to feel comfortable when our kids were at their house? It could be, of course, that we have done nothing wrong and that our child has simply chosen to be rebellious.

This type of self-analysis can be painful at times, but we owe it to ourselves and our families to engage in it not in order to place blame or to make anyone feel guilty but to determine the boundaries of our own responsibility. We certainly want to do all we can to prevent this kind of scenario from happening again and to put the details in perspective in an attempt to determine how it could have occurred in the first place. A behavioral crisis in any family would make the parents angry, frustrated, and disappointed. Yet this exercise in self-examination can help us understand the anger to some degree and to remain objective and rational, willing to look at the picture from every possible angle. This will help us to discard that first picture—the one that no longer fits the circumstances—and cling instead to the one that represents our new reality. The second picture can become as good as the first when we allow ourselves to look at it through the lens of forgiveness, without holding grudges.

Realize also that not everything needs to change at once and that a family doesn't deserve to be labeled unhealthy purely on the basis of the crisis. In fact, it is quite possible that a family that has experienced this kind of crossroads may emerge healthier for it. To arrive at that point, though, requires that everyone involved be willing to shoulder accountability for their own roles and that the family as a whole resolves to work as one cohesive unit to address the consequences and develop a plan of action.

What may hold parents back from recovering is the guilt and shame they feel that anything happened in the first place. But remember that Jesus is omniscient. He already knows everything that is going to happen. He isn't surprised when a crisis ensues. He knows that we all fall short of the glory of God and that we will until we are with Him in heaven. Therefore, God doesn't expect perfection from us. It doesn't mean we shouldn't strive to always do the right thing and be the best version of ourselves, but we also can't continually dwell over every wrong thing that happens or for any poor decisions we or someone in our family makes. We must learn to let go and let God.

TRUTH

Do not be anxious about anything, but in every situation, by prayer and petition, with thanksgiving, present your requests to God. And the peace of God, which transcends all understanding, will guard your hearts and your minds in Christ Jesus.
PHILIPPIANS 4:6–7

Isn't that how we feel about our children? We don't want to think they are going to fall short in any areas—after all, we take so many precautions to protect them—but it is unrealistic for us to assume that they won't mess up. We may know that intuitively, but we can't foresee how and when or to what degree they may make a disastrous decision. We can only continue to do our best to train them in the way they should go. And when a crisis does arise, we can, like Jesus, respond to them in love and help them find the way to handle this altered reality that will benefit all of us the most. Even though nothing about our predicament seems simple, we can take three basic steps toward handling our dilemma:

• *Mourn.* Parents need to take the time to mourn the loss of what could have been—the dream or expectation for our child that no longer fits.
• *Modify.* Once we have mourned, it is time to modify. This may entail making adjustments in our attitude, actions, and the roles we will play in the handling of the altered circumstances. It is important for us as parents to demonstrate flexibility and a willingness to change for the good of all.
• *Make peace.* After we have mourned our loss and made modifications, it is time for us to make peace with and accept the situation. We have committed ourselves to the reality represented by the new picture and are ready to move forward with our family under this new paradigm and to continue, both individually and as a unit, to grow and heal.

HOPE CHANGES EVERYTHING

Typically, in a crisis those involved have a difficult time seeing beyond it. A common response is for families to become consumed with it, perhaps feeling frozen and nonfunctional.

We must accept finite disappointment,
but we must never lose infinite hope.
MARTIN LUTHER KING JR.

Every family needs to keep in reserve a supply of hope to see them beyond the current circumstances when things go unexpectedly sour. Where does hope come from? This may not strike you as intuitive, but I believe that taking responsibility—as a lifestyle choice, not simply a response when a need arises—instills hope. When we have equipped ourselves in this way, we can survey that unforeseen situation with an eye toward resolution, as opposed to focusing solely on how and why the crisis has occurred. A solution will invariably involve a plan of some kind, goals, and eventually the glimpse of a light at the end of the tunnel. That is the kind of responsibility that breeds hope; we will feel much more readily that we know where we need to go and believe we *can* get there. If we refuse to accept responsibility, focusing instead on assigning blame, we stagnate and infuse no hope into the picture. Hope breeds a future; it is intrinsic to moving forward in life, whether or not a roadblock stands in our way.

Hope can also be gained by talking to someone who has successfully navigated a similar crisis. Only then can we start to realize that life is bigger than any one particular problem and that it will continue on both despite and following the disaster. Not allowing our lives to be defined by one event is critical; rather, each person involved must acknowledge the crisis as a part of her or his life—hopefully, though perhaps only in hindsight, as an aspect that reveals and showcases the strength of character.

A PICTURE FROM ABOVE

If you have ever flown in an airplane and sat near a window, you probably glanced out occasionally to enjoy the view. When we fly above the clouds, we have an opportunity to observe not only the rainy weather but the sunshine above the cloud cover. That ray of hope we glimpse in the distance assures us that something positive is coming. If we were rooted to the ground at that moment in time, we would see only the darkness and the pummeling rain. It wouldn't occur to us to hope for clearer skies, because our perspective would be based on the current negative reality.

When we catch a vision for a reality that lies beyond our immediate situation, that glimpse can infuse our spirits with a glimmer of confidence and assurance. Hope is a mental picture of what something *could* look like. If we have experienced the death of someone in our immediate family, we will likely benefit from the example of another family who has lost someone but is now thriving and happy once again; we will come to understand that this kind of resolution, even if not immediate, is possible. If our teenage daughter is pregnant, we might find hope in seeing another teen girl who has dealt with a pregnancy and is now living a successful and productive life.

Finding a support or care group that would match the needs of our particular situation could put us in touch with other people who have been on a similar journey. Sharing our story with trusted friends could also lead us to others who have experienced what we are going through. When we find out that we are not the only family to have walked through a particular valley, we can begin to reach out for the hope others may be eager to offer. As American poet Robert Frost once observed, "In three words I can sum up everything I have learned about life: it goes on." When we engage in conversation with others and learn how they have coped and survived, we start to realize that life does indeed go on. We embrace those first glimmerings of hope.

I can cite several prominent people who have endured a crisis when they were young adults and whose turnaround and success have been remarkable. Actor Tim Allen, who became famous for his hit shows *Home Improvement* and *Last Man Standing*, spent more than two years in federal prison for selling cocaine. The experience impelled him to turn his life around and to revive his stagnant stand-up comedy career.

Mark Wahlberg, who has appeared in more than two dozen movies and is the youngest of nine children, grew up having to fight for whatever he wanted. When his parents divorced, he took to hanging with a bad crowd. At thirteen years of age, he developed an addiction to cocaine, and at fourteen he dropped out of school. His lowest point came when, at sixteen, he was charged with attempted murder for beating a Vietnamese refugee with a metal hook, leaving the victim blind. Sentenced to two years in prison, he served only forty-five days, but during that short stay behind bars, he realized that his life was spiraling out of control and that he needed to change. He turned to his parish priest, who guided him back to the straight and narrow. Shortly thereafter Mark joined his brother's band, New Kids on the Block, and in early adulthood was catapulted to fame.

Bethany Hamilton is a professional surfer who became an inspiration to millions through her story of determination and faith. At the age of thirteen, Bethany lost her arm during a shark attack, but she never lost either her indomitable spirit or her desire to surf. Only a month after the attack, she returned to the water, and two years later she won her first national title. Bethany wrote a book about her life, which was adapted into a movie. She is now a wife and mother, as well as a motivational speaker touching the lives of millions of young girls.

More than participating in support groups and sharing

our story with others, we need to make certain our hope is anchored securely in Jesus Christ. It is one thing to read motivational stories or to share experiences with others who have overcome adversity, but in the final analysis, only Jesus Christ will see us and our family through a catastrophe.

WALKING A MILE IN THEIR SHOES

When Jim was young, he was a hard-core partier, especially in high school and college. Succumbing to the pressures of his peers, he experimented with drugs, alcohol, and sex. He didn't think much about the consequences of anything he did; he was just interested in acting cool around his friends and being popular. Jim managed to maintain good grades in school but was not as disciplined in his social life. Fortunately, he never experienced any serious consequences from his reckless behavior, although at times he came extremely close. He impregnated a girl he was dating, but she ended up experiencing a miscarriage during her second month.

Today Jim is a successful entrepreneur who is married with three teenage children. As a result of his own experiences, Jim has been strict with his children. Not taking into account the pressures they may be facing, he dictates rules and regulations to which he expects his kids to adhere—leaving them no allowance for error. Jim has difficulty recalling how he felt during his youth and consequently has little empathy for his children. While his intentions are admirable in that he is trying to prevent his children from engaging in risky behavior, his approach is unrealistic.

When his daughter came home pregnant at the age of seventeen, Jim was both angry and unsympathetic. Unable or unwilling to comprehend how she could have allowed this to happen, he has refused to talk to her about it. His daughter is distraught, and his wife is uncertain what to do. The family is in crisis, and each individual's reaction is only making things worse.

Jim's insensitive response is not uncommon, but it is anything but helpful to his daughter. Although he has reason to be angry, disappointed, and even shocked by the circumstances, he lacks empathy for how she or anyone else in the family may be feeling. Self-absorbed and unwilling to give an inch in the situation, he knows experientially what it is like to be a teenager in love but refuses to acknowledge those feelings to enable the family to move forward in dealing with the predicament.

Empathy requires parents to love their children both with their heads and with their hearts. It is about a willingness to look beyond our own hurt and anger and to move into the ability to care about the other person's pain. No, this doesn't come naturally; it requires a concerted effort on our part to try to understand how our child might be feeling—especially in light of the fact that we ourselves were once children and teenagers. This is a time when we need to set aside our personal feelings and start to consider what we could do to move the situation forward.

What lingers from a parent's individual past, unresolved or incomplete, often becomes part of her or his irrational parenting.
VIRGINIA SATIR

Imagine that the earthly Jesus' response to us when we were going through a crisis had been to turn His back and refuse to listen or help. What if He'd had no empathy for the ways in which we are tempted to sin? We know that Jesus came to earth in human form precisely so that He could be tempted and experience empathy with us over what we face. In Matthew 4:1–11 we read the story of Jesus' temptation in the wilderness. Notice that in response to every testing He faced, He struck back with the Word of God and overcame the temptation. The same formula will work for us. For every temptation, for every reckless behavior, for every adverse situation we face, we can turn to the Word of God for an answer!

STEPS TO EMPATHY

1. Set aside your own feelings, thoughts, and emotions for a time.
2. Vicariously envision yourself in the situation

and think about how you would feel if this circumstance were happening to you.

3. Communicate your understanding to the person, using statements that express how you think you might have felt in her or his situation.

4. Listen as that person responds to your explanation.

To help you physically enter the spirit of empathy, try actually walking around in a pair of the other person's shoes. You will see that vicariously interjecting yourself into someone else's situation can be tough, but at the same time you will gain a better appreciation for the situation overall.

If we don't learn the art of empathy we will never get past ourselves. Our focus will continue to be on how the crisis is affecting us, as opposed to how we and the others involved might together navigate through it. Empathy is one way for us to get outside ourselves and into the lives of our children, enabling us to parent them effectively through the difficult situation. Without empathy we won't see beyond our own reflection in the mirror and will consequently end up hurting not only ourselves but our family members as well.

FORGIVE AND FORGET

Forgiving and forgetting are never easy when someone we love has hurt us. Even though they may plead tearfully about how sorry they are, we may find it difficult to erase whatever has caused the pain. Compare this scenario to writing on a large whiteboard. You use a dry-erase marker to write something on the board, and when you are done, you try to erase it. A single clean sweep of your arm removes some of the coloring, after which a more vigorous up-and-down motion manages to delete a little more, but every time you look at the board, you see traces of where the marks had been.

That is how it can be when we try to forgive. Our child does something that hurts both us and them, and the family is in crisis as a result. The child comes to us sobbing and apologizing, and despite some internal resistance, we offer a semblance of forgiveness—which at that early juncture might be no more than words. The consequences of the reckless behavior litter the once-pristine emotional landscape in every direction, and even though we feel as though we have forgiven, relationships remain complicated. We continue to glimpse traces of the hurtful event everywhere we look; while we would like to let go of the situational aftermath, we can't completely erase the feelings from our mind. We simply aren't there yet.

Forgiveness can be about as comfortable for us as wearing a pair of pants that are too small—and about as natural as getting a child to eat tofu. The bottom line is that forgiveness is difficult and won't happen unless we make a conscious effort. When it comes to forgiving those we love the most and who love us back just as fiercely, letting go of a hurt can be even more of a challenge. The personal affront we feel is more intense than if a mere friend or acquaintance had wronged us.

Forgiveness involves a change of heart, not of circumstances. Nothing that can be spoken can be taken back, and the poor decision that was already made can't be rescinded nor the consequences eliminated. We are left with the choice either to ignore everything, letting the anger and disappointment fester inside until they boil over, or to deal with the situation, forgive the person who has injured us, and move forward in tandem.

Offering forgiveness immediately to avoid further conflict may be tempting, but that will only lead to pent-up anger, resentment, and false emotions if not done with sincerity. As we walk through and deal with the situation, we simply need to keep forgiveness in the forefront of our consciousness so that it will help us to remember it should ultimately be our goal.

Forgiveness was at the heart of Jesus, and as such, it is the foundation of the entire Gospel. God sacrificed His only Son for the forgiveness of our sins—past, present, and future. Why then do we struggle so much to forgive our children? Parenting with Jesus as our relational model has to include forgiveness! In Matthew 6:15 our Lord is quoted as saying, "If you do not forgive others their sins, your Father will not forgive your sins." Jesus and forgiveness are at the heart of navigating any crisis or adversity.

FORGIVENESS. . .

- is an ongoing process, not a one-time event,
- can be one-sided and still be successful, and
- can be obstructed by anger and bitterness.

A family that navigates a crisis well is a family characterized by forgiveness. A family can experience a crisis without necessarily dealing with a single definitive event. Circumstances can leave them living within a chronic and ongoing daily crisis. An example might be living through the relentless challenge of blending two families. Not only are there issues with the children trying to come to grips with a new stepparent—and possibly new stepsiblings—in their lives; there may also be an ongoing threat of potential backlash from ex-spouses who harbor resentment and hostility.

GETTING GOOD AT FORGIVENESS

If we want to become good at anything, we need to practice. Consider the daily regimen required of top sports figures and entertainers; they haven't arrived at their positions without hard work and practice. The same principle can be applied to forgiveness. If we want to be good at it, we have got to practice forgiving statements. Some such phrases include these:

- "I am sorry."
- "I was wrong about. . ."

- "I was wrong."
- "I will try not to do that again."
- "I didn't mean to hurt you. Will you forgive me?"

Becoming a great forgiver requires humility, and that means that pride will have to take a backseat. In fact, forgiving someone is more about laying down our own pride and releasing ourselves emotionally than it is about pardoning the other person's offense. That is part of the mix, but it isn't the primary impetus behind forgiveness. If our child sees us as stubbornly withholding our pardon, the chances are our hesitation will hurt *us* more in the long run than it will the one seeking absolution. Even though we may have been the one wronged, our choice to suppress forgiveness will become the thorn that repeatedly pricks within the relationship. Our example of practicing forgiveness will be the one our children follow, and our ability and willingness to forgive will be the determining factors in how the crisis is resolved.

ARE YOU READY TO BE COMMITTED?

Negotiating parenthood may at times make us think we should be committed. . .to an institution. Kids have a pernicious tendency to drive their parents crazy. As we talk about families working through a crisis, though, the reference is to making a commitment to do whatever it takes to get everyone safely through the difficult time.

Making a commitment implies our intention to follow through on what we say we will do. In today's society, people break "commitments" all the time—which negates the claim that these stated or implied promises qualified as commitments in the first place. What many people offer, far from being a pledge or promise, is closer to a halfhearted agreement that may get trumped if something more enticing comes along or our fickle emotions or altered circumstances lead us in an alternate direction.

To navigate a crisis successfully, everybody in the family has to resolve to make the intended resolution work, to do whatever it takes to ensure that all involved come through intact. If one person bails, their noncompliance with the plan will disrupt the harmony and violate established trust, leaving the entire effort to dissipate into thin air. When we make a pact with one another, we do so trusting and believing that each individual will fulfill her or his side of the bargain.

If a child gets into trouble because she is caught drinking on school grounds, she may get expelled. The parents' part of navigating the crisis includes establishing new ground rules for that child to follow, and part of the child's response is a commitment to abide by those rules, which include a strict prohibition on drinking alcohol. Imagine that your child is out one night at a party with friends. The temptation to drink proves irresistible, and she comes home with alcohol on her breath. Trust has been broken—the commitment shattered. The family essentially finds itself in crisis mode all over again. This means that all of the associated steps—accepting and taking responsibility, finding hope, exercising empathy, practicing forgiveness, and committing to succeed—have to be repeated. It could take several more tries before the family is functioning effectively again, but such recommitment will always prove worthwhile. Never give up on your family!

TRUTH IN THE WORD

When God the Father is invited in as part of the equation, no family needs to shoulder the burden of a crisis on their own. Every step is supported by a scripture nugget to which we can cling for comfort. The apostle Paul functioned as a terrific example of supporting others. Again and again he used his gifts of encouragement and leadership to raise up mature believers and evangelists for Christ. God intends for us to help and support each other throughout life—skills and commitments that are especially necessary when we are enduring a tough situation.

When it comes to ownership of responsibility, Paul points out in Romans 14:12 that "each of us will give an account of ourselves to God." And in Hebrews 4:13 we are reminded that "nothing in all creation is hidden from God's sight. Everything is uncovered and laid bare before the eyes of him to whom we must give account." In every situation, the parties involved must take some responsibility, even when some of those involved had no control over how and why the crisis happened. God is observing our response. If we sit back smugly and simply pass judgment, we, too, will be implicated. "Do not judge," cautioned Jesus, "or you too will be judged. For in the same way you judge others, you will be judged, and with the measure you use, it will be measured to you" (Matthew 7:1–2).

We can thrive if we have hope, a component of faith. In fact, hope is one of the foundations on which we stand. As Hebrews 11:1 reminds us, "Faith is confidence in what we hope for and assurance about what we do not see." Hope is what we need when faced with a devastating situation; without it we have precisely nothing. "And hope does not put us to shame, because God's love has been poured out into our hearts through the Holy Spirit, who has been given to us" (Romans 5:5).

Empathy, so prevalent in the Bible, is illustrated in the transformation of Saul to Paul. Jesus converts a man who was even then engaged in the public persecution of Christians. Paul's ensuing ministry is based on his own infamous suffering and persecution as a Christian. Who better to understand both positions than this one who had walked in the persecutor's sandals? Jesus asks us to carry each other's burdens, which we can do more effectively when we understand how the other person is thinking and feeling about the situation. In Galatians 6:2 Paul directs his readers to "carry each other's burdens and in this way you will fulfill the law of Christ."

Forgiveness is supernatural. It is difficult to forgive in our own strength because offering pardon is counterintuitive for us. When we have been wronged, we naturally want to strike back or pull away. This is especially true when a hurt is bigger than ourselves or the other person, as in the case when someone has injured our child, either on purpose or by accident. In Matthew 18:21–22 Jesus and Peter discuss forgiveness. "Then Peter came to Jesus and asked, 'Lord, how many times shall I forgive my brother or sister who sins against me? Up to seven times?' Jesus answered, 'I tell you not seven times, but seventy-seven times.' "

Commitment is equally important in marriage and in our relationship with God, who asks us several times in the Bible to commit our hearts. In Psalm 37:5 each of us is directed to "commit your way to the LORD; trust in him." And in 1 Kings 8:61 we read, " 'May your hearts be fully committed to the LORD our God, to live by his decrees and obey his commands.' " We are to do the same in our families, committing ourselves to each other so that we will do whatever it takes to stay together and work out whatever conflicts might arise. This is what Jesus would have done and even now continues to do with us every day.

QUESTIONS TO CONSIDER

1. The first step in navigating a crisis is to take responsibility for whatever role we may have played in the event.

   What does it mean to you to take responsibility in a crisis?

2. Every family needs hope in order to see beyond current circumstances.

   How can you find hope in the midst of a crisis?

3. Empathy requires parents to love their children with both their heads and their hearts.

   How would you rate your current level of empathy?
   What steps can you take to improve this level?

4. Forgiveness is difficult and won't happen unless you make a conscious effort.

   How easily do you tend to forgive your children?
   What can you do to strengthen your ability and willingness to forgive?

5. As Hebrews 11:1 reminds us, "Faith is confidence in what we hope for and assurance about what we do not see."

   What part does your faith play in dealing with a crisis?

DAN'S REALITY CHECK

A crisis managed well is a blessing in disguise. It might not feel like a blessing when you are in the thick of it, but it will strengthen your character and resolve. It will also help you mature and grow in love. Quite possibly the way you handle a situation will set a good example for someone else.

CHAPTER 5

The Truth about Effective Parenting

Measuring the effectiveness of our parenting is difficult. In some cases, as when we talk to our kids about an inappropriate behavior and it stops, we can see immediate results. But when a child chooses that same behavior again, five minutes or two weeks later, parents are left to wonder whether their parenting has been successful. Unfortunately, this roller coaster between confidence and satisfaction on the one hand, and doubt and indecision on the other will probably continue until our children become adults. And even then, as we watch them continue to progress and mature, we will continue to question whether their behavior and the choices they are making may have had something to do with the way we parented them.

But that is just one side of the equation. When we see positive responses to our parenting and our children begin to learn how to live and behave like mature adults who make wise and informed decisions, we will also wonder whether this observable outcome is a direct reflection of the effectiveness of our parenting. We, as parents, tend to accept blame more easily than we accept credit.

DISCIPLINING FOR EFFECT

Discipline is one of the vehicles we use to steer our children down the road of right behavior and sound judgment. It is part of the way we go about speaking truth into our children's lives. We employ discipline in the hope of seeing a positive outcome in our children. Disciplining children is a long, winding road with seemingly endless hills, dips, curves, and potholes that are sure to challenge our skills and confidence. The road stretches out from infancy all the way through to adulthood. Our job as parents is to chart a course that incorporates several different methods of discipline, all of which are appropriate for each child at every stage of his development.

The child supplies the power, but the parents have to do the steering.
BENJAMIN SPOCK

For discipline to have the desired effect, a child at any age needs to feel unconditionally loved. The love factor is more important than anything else. A child who knows and experiences this type of security will accept discipline more readily and will be more likely to achieve a healthy self-esteem, the ability to build and sustain relationships, and ultimately the capacity to integrate and maintain rules in his own life for all the right reasons. The culmination of employing equal parts of truth and grace will create a healthy environment in which a child can grow into a responsible adult.

TRUTH

Whoever spares the rod hates their children, but the one who loves their children is careful to discipline them.
PROVERBS 13:24

PARENTING INFLUENCES

Your parenting methods are likely to reflect the way you were parented. The dominant parenting style in the early and middle part of the twentieth century tended to be controlling and authoritarian. Punishments for nonperformance and disobedience were harsh, and the governing theme that prevailed in most homes was a belief that children would flourish only through punishment for any infringement. Thus the experience of childhood for many children of that era mirrored more closely that of a boot camp than of a loving family. Although most grew up to be functional adults, their personalities may have been stifled to some degree and their capacity for flexibility and reasoning hampered.

As we entered the latter part of the twentieth century and continue to move further into the twenty-first, more varied parenting styles have emerged, all of which tend to be less domineering and more permissive and indulgent, resulting in children who tend to be more self-centered. In addition, the entire family structure has changed dramatically since the 1950s, from a typical two-parent home in which the mom stayed home and the dad worked outside the home to a medley of scenarios today that include children being raised by working moms, single parents, stepparents, and even grandparents and other relatives. These changes have greatly impacted the manner in which we parent our kids. Many complicating factors make parenting more challenging than before, though certainly not impossible. Now, more than ever before, we must make the effort to evaluate how, and how effectively, we are parenting.

THE INFLUENCE OF MEDIA

Television sitcoms are often a barometer of the way in which society views families and parenting. In the 1950s, programs like *The Adventures of Ozzie and Harriet* illustrated the then-traditional family values. This wholesome sitcom featured a two-parent, middle-class suburban family whose days were filled with peace, love, and laughter. *Leave It to Beaver* was a similar show that featured clever children and loving parents. The 1970s ushered in sitcoms that began reflecting changes in the family and the world. *All in the Family* depicted a brasher side of parenting, and *The Brady Bunch* introduced America to one of the first stepfamilies on television. Still today it remains one of the most influential sitcoms of all time.

The decade of the '80s rolled in, bringing with it situation comedies like *Different Strokes*, which featured African American siblings who had been adopted by an upper-class single white father. *Married with Children*, centering around family dysfunction, debuted as the polar opposite of shows from the 1950s; the cast included a deadbeat dad, a frustrated and lazy housewife, and two sexually charged children.

In the 1990s, the American family was portrayed through shows like *Full House*, in which a widower was helped by his brother-in-law and a best friend to raise his three children. In *Fresh Prince of Bel-Air*, a young man living in an undesirable neighborhood in Philadelphia was shipped away by his concerned mom to live with his affluent uncle in Bel-Air, California. This era also brought us *Home Improvement*, which featured a traditional two-parent family raising three boys. The multitude of family dynamics portrayed through these shows characterized the ever-increasing complexity of parenting, and of society in general.

As we entered the twenty-first century, television executives seemed to give up on creating make-believe families, opting instead to film real-life families going about their days, and viewers can't seem to get enough. *The Bachelor* and *The Bachelorette* have redefined how singles date. *The Real Housewives of Orange County* and *The Real Housewives of New Jersey* share far too much information and drama. These extreme examples of real life can be so outrageous that we may think we are viewing fiction. Despite the popularity of reality TV, there is still an audience that appreciates the networks' attempts to create fictional families that try to reflect real-world trends.

While these television sitcoms are seemingly harmless, the danger lies in the underlying pressure they exert on parents who, as an outcome of viewing them, feel as though they are doing something wrong. Numerous themes and messages relayed through the dialogue and scenes seem to retract the clear principles of God's Word, but because we see these scenarios played out on television or in movies—often humorously so—we may at times be tempted to question our beliefs or downplay our standards. While I am certainly not advocating that we avoid watching either television or movies, I am cautioning Christian viewers to tread lightly, remaining intentionally aware of how these shows may affect our thinking or, as I discussed in chapter 2, stealing our normal.

IDENTIFYING YOUR PARENTING STYLE

The parents in situation comedies, like those in real life, reveal a style of parenting based on the manner in which they discipline and interact with their children. Most of us don't pause to think about or identify our parenting styles, but if someone were to observe our parenting over a period of time, a clear style would emerge. For the most part, parents are too busy acting and reacting to their children to consider whether they are exemplifying a style. Still, if each of us would evaluate the disciplinary techniques we use with our children, we could determine whether that style is the most beneficial for them. Although one could argue that there is no intrinsically right or wrong style of parenting, there is a preferred style that will last throughout the ages because it isn't dependent on trends or people. I hope you will bear with my keeping you in suspense long enough to review the various styles researchers have identified over the years.

AUTHORITARIAN STYLE

Most people are familiar with what is known as the authoritarian style of parenting. This is the "my way or the highway" approach to discipline. While certainly an effective style for a parent who always wants to have his or her way, it often leaves children feeling insecure, convinced that only model performance will earn them love. This is a performance-based acceptance style, in that the amount of love people receive is believed to be directly commensurate with how well they perform. Examples of an authoritarian style of parenting might include the following:

- being rigidly strict and lacking communication with children
- continuously reminding children of who is in charge
- punishing children for not following the rules while failing to communicate expectations or the consequences if those expectations are not met

PERMISSIVE STYLE

Children whose parents are permissive in nature may be having the time of their lives—or so they think. The reality is, though, that without boundaries children flounder. They struggle with managing their behavior, as well as with adhering to the structures imposed on them by other people, such as teachers or employers. Permissive parents often try to be more like a friend than a parent. Examples of permissive parenting include these:

- failure to discipline children when they disobey
- wanting to be a child's best friend
- preferring compromise to conflict with children

TRUTH

*"Those whom I love I rebuke and discipline.
So be earnest and repent."*
REVELATION 3:19

HELICOPTER PARENTING STYLE

Helicopter parenting is a familiar term that is somewhat self-explanatory, stemming from a picture of the parent who constantly "hovers" over his or her children, almost to the point of smothering. While parents are responsible for the safety and security of their children, too much protection can render children tentative or afraid to take risks in life. This could interfere with their realizing the plans God has for them. Examples of this style include the following:

- rarely letting children make age-appropriate decisions
- rarely allowing children to be out of sight
- attempting to control every aspect of children's lives, even when they are capable of handling situations on their own

UNINVOLVED PARENTING STYLE

This term is also self-explanatory, referring to a style in which the parent is uninvolved and/or distant, possibly bordering on neglectful. Children may feel insecure and unloved but are forced by circumstances to take on greater responsibility than they are truly capable of handling. This type of parenting may include the following:

- leaving children alone regularly to rely on themselves
- showing little or no interest in children's friends

or the places they hang out
- frequently making excuses for an alleged need to be away from children

Do you see yourself in any of these descriptions? It may be that you borrow a little from one or more of these styles. But if you are looking for an optimal style of parenting, one designed specifically with children in mind, try the Jesus style. Our Lord created the world and everything in it and, of course, in His infinite wisdom and love, He inspired the various biblical writers to compose a manual that would cover all of the situations we face in life and in parenting. That doesn't mean we can't learn and grow from exposure to other resources as well, but all of the information we take in should be funneled and filtered through God's vision.

THE JESUS STYLE

The Jesus style of parenting is the perfect style because Jesus alone is perfect! As Christians we ought to be familiar with this style because it is the design under which we live as God's adopted children. We may not always emulate or execute it perfectly, but that doesn't change the quality of the style. The Jesus style exemplifies the precise balance of what children need—grace and truth!

The Jesus style incorporates love, discipline, care, and protection. An important first step in following this style is that of communicating age-appropriate expectations to your children as they grow, beginning as soon as they are old enough to understand. Children need and in reality even crave boundaries. They need to know ahead of time our expectations in all areas of life, as well as what will happen if they fail to meet them.

You don't have to look very hard in the Bible to get started. The Ten Commandments, which God gave to Moses initially as guidelines for the Israelites, outline the basic tenets of responsible godly behavior. At the time, God's people were being easily led astray into inappropriate conduct. Because God loved them—and each of us—so much, He provided the commandments as a foundation from which His people are to operate.

Just as Moses communicated those commandments to the Israelites, parents need to communicate expectations to their children. Left on their own without guidance, children will make poor choices—candy for breakfast, midnight for bedtime, and a 4:00 a.m. curfew. When we create boundaries that speak to their well-being, our children will feel loved and be confident that someone cares enough about them to want to know what—and how—they are doing. The same dynamic is at work when we experience peace and joy in the knowledge that God cares about how and what we are doing.

Those who view the Ten Commandments as restrictive might appreciate them more if they were to understand why God put them into place. As an example, God knew that adultery would be intensely hurtful, destructive to everyone involved. There is nothing glamorous or sexy about this choice, even though it may be portrayed that way in the media. God knows the damage adultery will cause and wants to protect us all from such harm. We can look at each commandment through this lens and in this way come to understand the motivation behind it. In a similar way, our children may at times see our boundaries as restrictive but will eventually perceive their value once they recognize the concern they manifest and the protection they provide. At some point, they will realize that we have rules because we love them.

The Israelites struggled with understanding the value of the commandments in much the same way our children, and especially our teenagers, fail to appreciate the value of our rules or expectations. The Israelites were obliged to wander in the desert for forty years because they couldn't grasp the concept of obedient living according to the commandments, and so they continuously tested God's authority. When we read about these ancient people today, we may wonder how they could have been so dense, how they could have messed up so habitually and predictably; everything seems so clear to us as we read about their situation more than three thousand years after the fact. We cringe in disbelief at what they did, despite the reality that we have all disobeyed God. And so will our children, who will disobey both God and their parents. We may have one or more children who accept discipline easily, while another may test our authority at every turn. The children who are resistant to our guidance may wander in the desert much longer than the others. I know. I have a child like that.

ANNA'S STORY—THE TRUTH

My youngest daughter, Anna, was such a child. Hers is the kind of tale I had honestly hoped I'd never have to share as a parent. But the Lord has called me to be honest and vulnerable about the areas in which I have experienced growth and learned some difficult and valuable lessons. What my wife and I experienced with Anna falls within that category. And with Anna's permission, I am able to share this story.

I have learned that balancing truth and grace when it comes to discipline is never easy. Having four children who are different in many ways posed a challenge for us to find the most effective disciplinary technique for each one. Some worked for all four of them, but certain situations required individualized approaches.

As a baby and toddler, Anna was the easiest of our children to raise. Fun and full of charisma, she was consistently the life of the party, quickly earning the nickname Bubbly. She brought such delight to our family. I can attest that parenting Anna with truth and grace in the early years was a piece of cake. She would actually come to me after she had misbehaved and announce, "Daddy, I think I deserve to be punished. What do we need to do?" She was a dream.

As Anna began to move into her teen years, however, that dream gradually morphed into a nightmare. We hosted a foreign exchange student in our home for a year when Anna was in high school, and that, coupled with ordinary family changes, created an environment in which some issues fell through the inevitable parenting cracks. Anna would disavow any connection, claiming that she simply chose at that point to rebel. When I describe her as rebellious, I am not talking about a girl who smart-mouthed us on occasion. Anna moved all the way to a place of disassociating with us as her parents, as well as with her siblings. In the depth of her revolt, she manifested a disrespectful attitude toward our property and belongings, ignored most of the boundaries we had put in place, and displayed a general disregard for anything resembling the way she had been raised. Her about-face was extremely painful and disheartening. After the older three had made it through their teens—not with perfection but certainly with respect and love—my wife and I felt as though we had been sucker punched. We were knocked off our feet.

During this time, I was regularly traveling and speaking, bringing the message of winning at home all across the country, when in reality I felt more like I was losing at home. Some days the only strength I could muster enabled me to do no more than put one foot in front of the other while chanting an internal refrain of "You can do this. You can do this." I would repeatedly recite Philippians 4:13 to myself: "I can do all things through Christ who strengthens me" (NKJV).

At the height of this nightmarish period, Anna moved away, declaring that she just needed space from us. In all honesty, we desperately needed space from her. She was also trying to break free from an extremely unhealthy relationship. I will never forget one of the phone calls I received from her during that time. She was out on the road driving when she called me and admitted in a small, pathetic voice, "Daddy, I'm lost." I remember counseling her, "Anna, look toward the sun! You will drive the right way if you are driving toward the sun." Looking back, this seemingly simple advice had so many spiritual overtones that I am amazed. How often have we as parents felt lost and cried out to our Father in heaven? And we read over and over again, in many contexts, in God's Word that we are to look to the "Son"— the Son of God.

We didn't see Anna on a daily basis anymore, and the separation was difficult. My wife and I experienced many sleepless nights, hours during which it seemed natural to lie awake and try to figure out what we had done well and where we had failed. I had certainly been too soft at times, which were strangely counterbalanced against instances when I'd been too harsh. Maybe I'd been too angry. . .or, then again, maybe not angry enough. This was the kind of situation that will make a parent second-guess all of his or her decisions and behavior.

I remember a couple of nights during which I sat alone and stared out a window on the back side of our home. I would gaze at the moon, notice how it reflected on the water, and seriously wonder whether I was going to make it. This was by far the most difficult season Jane and I had experienced in all our years of parenting. Following (unfiltered and in no particular order!) is a catalog of some of the thoughts that flitted regularly through my troubled mind during those nights I spent alone at the height of my daughter's defiance.

MY THOUGHTS

Hopeless

Not knowing what to do

Stomach in a knot and mind in torture

Alone

Desperate for God to intervene

Desiring to be holy

Desiring to be earnest in my prayers

Wanting to be more committed to believing that
        Christ is the answer

Angry

Worried whether my daughter was still alive

Righteously angry

Somewhat embarrassed, but not as much as I might
        have anticipated

Determined to believe that God was seeing some-
        thing bigger than me

Small, insignificant, and humble

As though I had failed at something

Hopeful and wanting to know the future

Wondering how my other children were affected by
        Anna's behavior

Knowing that in about thirty years none of this
        would matter

Wanting Christ to return

Wanting to move back to the Carolinas, buy a trailer,
        and live out my last years quietly

Imagining that some were enjoying their observation
        of my predicament

Not sure of what was going to happen and convinced
that the uncertainty was killing me
Know I should be doing what I advise others to do—
let go and let God
Amazed at how this once joyful little girl could have
become so defiant
Frustrated at my apparent inability to say anything
that might positively affect the situation
Ready to give up, throw in the towel, raise the white
flag
Acknowledging that the spiritual battle in which we
are engaged is not of this world
Completely at the mercy of God
Missing my little girl immensely
Desiring to scream, punch, and knock the crap out of
something, even though this wouldn't help
Wishing I could think clearly and focus on other
things
Wanting to take my own life and just be done with
it all
Disjointed, my thoughts were scattered
Wondering how people like Jesus and Job had man-
aged to withstand their testing
Listening more closely than ever before and hearing
the Lord speak to me
Knowing I needed to keep myself busy but wanting
to do absolutely nothing
Willing to let Jesus Christ shape me through this
experience

Yet somehow through and in spite of it all, God sustained me, assuring me that I would soon be teaching on this very subject and that my experience-based words would help others grow and provide much-needed encouragement for them. He instructed me not to walk away discouraged, because my testing was nearly complete. Then He reminded me that He gives us not "a spirit of fear, but of power and of love and of a sound mind" (2 Timothy 1:7 NKJV). He directed me to trust Him, pledging that He would give my wife and me profound relief.

God also reminded me that many of His children have rebelled. This realization drew me to people in the Bible like Adam and Eve, Saul, David, and Samson. God had not only continued to love them after their falls but had used them afterward for His greater glory. And just as God shows us through the example of these Bible giants of His unconditional love, I assured my daughter, "You are my child, and you will never be able to separate yourself from that fact. I will always love you, no matter what happens, but right now I can't financially support you because of your behavior and the choices you are making." This was one of the most difficult parenting decisions Jane and I ever had to make. There were times when Anna didn't have food and would call her mom for help. I would get on the phone and cry with her, but I would also explain that helping would only enable her to continue in her poor choices—something I loved her too much to condone.

God responds to us in much the same way. When we sin we are rebelling against Him, and during that period of defiance, God can't help us unless we focus on seeking release from the grip of sin. Anna wasn't asking for assistance in abandoning the lifestyle she had chosen; what she wanted was for us to support her in that lifestyle. As a loving Father, I couldn't do that, just as God won't do that with us.

ANNA'S STORY—THE GRACE

Anna has now returned home, and the situation is measurably better. We aren't perfect parents, and Anna isn't a perfect daughter, but we have all learned a great deal about grace and truth. I have learned a lot about grace and she about truth, but the reverse is also true in both directions.

Several months after Anna had returned home, I met with a couple in my office who were seeking counsel on handling a situation with one of their children who had gone astray. I shared with them a little of Anna's story. For some reason, my daughter was in the office that day, and as she walked by, I pointed her out to them. They asked for permission to speak to her, and I called her into the room. After an initial greeting, Anna agreed to answer their questions.

The first was simply "What should we do?" Anna looked directly into the eyes of these distraught parents and responded, "First of all, don't blame yourself. My mom and dad didn't do everything right, but this isn't on them. It is on me. These were my decisions. My mom and dad held the line and made me realize they weren't going to compromise their moral standards in our home. That is one of the things that made me want to go back there. So don't blame yourself if your child chooses to rebel. That decision is on them."

"I do believe that by balancing grace with truth; by speaking godly principles into my daughter's life, even when she didn't want to hear them; by praying for her; by seeking to honor Jesus; and by modeling a good example in our home and family, I helped pave the way for Anna's return."

Next Anna advised the couple to let their child go, explaining that the more they fought to get her attention, the more she would pull away. If they let her go, the chance of her returning would be greater.

Finally, Anna counseled them, "Make sure you continue to pray and seek God for wisdom"—this from the very person who had chosen to create the distancing and the drama!

Though I could have done a lot of things better, I hadn't made the decision for us to separate. Anna had. I do believe, however, that by balancing grace with truth; by speaking godly principles into my daughter's life, even when she didn't want to hear them; by praying for her; by seeking to honor Jesus; and by modeling a good example in our home and family, I helped pave the way for Anna's return.

One day after she had been home for a while, I asked her, "Anna, what was the turning point that made you decide to come home?" Her answer was simple: "I woke up at 3:30 one morning, after sleeping outside on a picnic table, and I thought to myself, *Why am I doing this when my parents have a home I can live in?*" Her answer reminded me immediately of the one given by the lost son in Jesus' parable recorded in Luke 15. One day, Jesus said, the son's eyes were opened and he asked himself, *Why am I living in a pigpen when my dad has a home where I can live?*

Many of you are going through a similar experience right now with one of your children. You are struggling with how to balance grace and truth. Tough love, though difficult, is necessary. Think about what Jesus would have said in response to your circumstances. Think about how Jesus would have responded to your daughter or son who is struggling in a wayward lifestyle. His grace would have been—and is!—incredibly powerful. He would have told your child how much He loved him and encouraged him to seek God first in all he did. He would have explained that although He couldn't support him if he continued to make wrong choices, He would never stop loving him. When Jesus pledges, "I will never leave you nor forsake you" (Hebrews 13:5 NKJV), He means that He will always be there waiting for an invitation to help.

Balancing truth and grace as you discipline is a process you will learn over time, but hopefully it will bring healing and hope to your family. As I have stated, although our current relationship with Anna isn't perfect, it is light-years ahead of where it used to be. I believe that one day God is going to use her story to shape a lot of lives, just as she has shaped mine.

TRUTH IN THE WORD

Enforcing discipline is one of the more difficult parental tasks. No mom or dad really enjoys it, even when a child is being extraordinarily obstinate! That is because we, as parents who have known our children since birth, can see past the behavior to the person within. So if you are wondering why disciplining your children is important, consider this nugget from Proverbs: "Do not withhold discipline from a child; if you punish them with the rod, they will not die. Punish them with the rod and save them from death" (23:13–14). God knows that a child who is never disciplined will never prosper in life. If you have asked yourself whether there should be consequences if your child disobeys, listen to Paul's inspired counsel: "Children, obey your parents in the Lord, for this is right" (Ephesians 6:1).

If we don't discipline our children for disobedience, we are failing to reinforce our Lord's command for their obedience. If we permit them to disobey us, they will never learn to obey God. Disciplining our children helps them grow into the people God created them to be. When we falter or decline to follow through on the task of raising the children God has assigned to us, *they* will suffer from our abdication. Unable to find their way into the will of God, they will have no means for becoming the people God has designed them to be. Yes, discipline is hard, especially when we feel as though we are the only parents doing it! But remember what the Father said and follow His normal. Parent your children in the same way

God parents you every day. "See what great love the Father has lavished on us, that we should be called children of God! And that is what we are!" (1 John 3:1).

QUESTIONS TO CONSIDER

1. Measuring the effectiveness of our parenting is difficult. In some cases, we may see immediate results because we talk to our kids about an inappropriate behavior and it stops. But when they choose that same behavior again, five minutes or two weeks later, we are left to wonder whether our parenting is effective.

    What is there about discipline that is most difficult for you?

2. Most of us don't pause to think about or identify our parenting styles, but if someone were to observe our parenting over a period of time, a clear style would emerge.

    Which parenting style—authoritarian, permissive, helicopter, uninvolved, or Jesus style—best defines your own? Explain why.

3. You may have one or more children who accept discipline easily, while another may test your authority at every turn. That child may wander in that desert much longer than the others.

    To what degree does this statement resonate with you, perhaps reminding you of one of your children?

4. Balancing truth and grace as you discipline is a process you will learn over time, but hopefully it will bring healing and hope to your family.

What one change are you considering in the way you discipline your children?

_____

DAN'S REALITY CHECK

You will probably continually question your style and methods of parenting all of your life, but if you try to use the Jesus style more often than not, it will serve you well in every situation. It is not a guarantee that everything will be perfect and that your children will be angelic, but it is a way for you to feel confident about your decisions and actions along with being more consistent in your parenting.

_____

CHAPTER 6

The Truth about Blended Families

Families come in all different shapes and sizes. There are single-parent families, stepfamilies, and two-parent families. There are families where children are being raised by grandparents, as well as families where all or some of the children are adopted. There are various reasons for the variety we see today in families. One of those is divorce. Although God never intended for couples to get divorced, we know that in a fallen world it happens. In Jesus' words in Matthew 19:4–6, "Haven't you read. . .that at the beginning the Creator 'made them male and female,' and said, 'For this reason a man will leave his father and mother and be united to his wife, and the two will become one flesh'? So they are no longer two, but one flesh. Therefore what God has joined together, let no one separate." God is also clear in stating through His prophet in Malachi 2:16 that He hates divorce—not the people who have been divorced but the idea or reality of marital dissolution.

God's motivation for His stance on divorce is straightforward: it hurts children and families. Period. Even when a follower of Christ has scriptural permission to divorce, the end result is going to be pain for all involved. Anyone who believes for a moment that divorce doesn't affect children, the separating couple, and even extended family members and friends, is being unrealistic. I recently attended a funeral service and was involved with a family that was dealing with all sorts of issues related to the burial of their loved one. A divorce within the family was causing conflict. One person spoke up, admitting, "I am divided." This situation convinces me even more that divorce stinks because it causes so much pain.

While the ideal goal is to avoid its happening at all, when divorce does occur, we need to pray and take steps to ensure that the children are affected as little as possible. We need to seek God's strength and wisdom in handling the situation, because as humans we will initially act selfishly in all matters concerning the divorce, especially when either or both parties feel they have been wronged in some way.

People who divorce, despite their best intentions to the contrary, tend to put their own needs before those of the children, believing they will adjust and be fine. I know this because it is human nature to think first of ourselves. I agree with what I once heard a pastor say about God's command to love our neighbors as ourselves—that God gave this command because He knew the extent to which we would love ourselves in a prideful way. He knew we would concentrate first on how everything affects *us*. God wants us to love others to that same degree. Think of your children as those "others" and consider how every decision surrounding the divorce will affect them. This will become all the more critical when dealing with stepparents or becoming a stepparent. It may be hard to muster tolerance—let alone love—for that new person in your child's life, or for you to love your new spouse's child, but God commands this. And we need to do so for the sake of our children. Because divorce was never God's intention, we won't find scripture passages that directly address stepparenting or blended families issues, but that doesn't mean we can't find help in God's Word to deal with those circumstances. While families can no longer be defined in one-size-fits-all terms, we can still raise our children God's way.

THE STATS

According to the website SmartStepfamilies.com, a whole lot of people are involved in a step relationship of one kind or another. An estimated one-third of children will live in a stepparent home before the age of eighteen, and 50 percent will have a stepparent at some point in their lifetime. Approximately one-third of all weddings in America today form stepfamilies, and an estimated 40 percent of women will live in a married or cohabiting stepfamily home at some point. Sixty-five percent of remarriages involve one or more children, meaning that there is more merging going on in families than on the highway! Forty-two percent of adults have a step relationship—either as a stepparent, a stepsibling, a half sibling, or a stepchild. That translates to nearly 100 million adults.

Statistics on the SmartStepfamilies.com website show that serial transitions in and out of marriage/divorce/cohabitation have become typical of family life in the United States. The data also claim that Americans marry, divorce, and cohabit more than those in any other Western society. In addition, the website reports that children living with two married parents in the United States run a higher risk of experiencing a family breakup than children living with two unmarried parents in Sweden! That is crazy and sad at the same time, but it is the reality of our society.

These research stats add up to a lot of families trying to assimilate, though, sadly—and this nuance is not included in the data—in all likelihood not blending well.

THE MAGIC OF BLENDING

The Magic Bullet is a clever blender–food processor invention that is handy for mixing food and liquids. I wish such a tool could be developed for blending families, but there is no magic to it. Although I don't live in a blended family in the way society defines the term, I have talked to many people who do—and in some sense I believe all families are blended in one way or another.

A "blended" family in the traditional sense consists of any two people who join in marriage, coming to the union with one or more children from a previous relationship to form a new family. Experts identify the keys to managing a blended family as communication, flexibility, and respect. This situation is not so different from that of a traditional family; it is all too easy for any of us to mix up these priorities.

There is no such thing as an "instant family." Forging bonds of love and trust takes time, whether the child is a biological descendant or comes to us through adoption or marriage. Too many remarried couples expect the love connection among all involved to be instantaneous. This isn't surprising in our instant-gratification society that expects nearly everything to be easy and immediate. Digital pictures, after all, are available within seconds, the internet is a click away, and the television springs to life at the press of a remote button. The most worthwhile relationships, however, take time and nurturing to develop and grow.

Part of the problem is the urgent desire of remarried couples for all their children to get along; they forget that their compatibility as a couple doesn't automatically translate to their children's compatibility. Couples struggling with the fine art of blending a family need to practice patience. Each spouse should get to know each of the other's children. Spend time together with them alone—and not just on holidays. Develop new traditions! And bear in mind that you as a stepparent are not a replacement mother or father as much as you are an additive to the mix (this applies even if the missing parent is no longer living or is otherwise unavailable except in memory). Think of yourself as someone who can flavor without spoiling that mix or trying to change the taste. Don't be threatened by the ongoing relationship the children may have with their other biological parent. And don't neglect to reassure your own children of your love when they see you forming bonds with their stepsiblings. It is natural for jealousy to occur, but it can be handled appropriately, with awareness and acknowledgment as critical first steps.

Keep in mind that even parents who are married struggle with differing, and at times conflicting, parenting styles. Then imagine the couple divorcing and other adult players, with their own individual parenting styles, being added to the stew. It is easy to see how that pot can get stirred up.

In my experience, a part of the reason blending families can be so difficult is that individuals allow their egos to drive the process instead of tucking them away in the trunk where they belong. The kids are expected simply to ride along, offering no input into any decisions—though directly affected by all of them. The decision to divorce. To remarry. To create a new family tree. I am not chastising those who make these life-changing choices but simply asking parents to try to conceptualize all that the kids involved have to process or simply accept. Try not to expect too much from them too soon in terms of your image of happily ever after.

If you lead with humility and empathy and allow the children to follow in their own time, incorporating many of the suggestions above, your new family will blend more smoothly, and hopefully you will begin to see fewer areas of separation.

BEYOND THE EGOS

There is no standard playbook in a stepfamily as to what involvement the stepparent should have in the lives of the children. Every family situation is different. Biological parents and stepparents need to work out roles that complement each other's and play to each other's strengths. Just as in homes with two biological (or adoptive) parents, parents and stepparents in a blended situation must be unified in goals and work together as a team. Stepparents who are struggling need biological parents who will step up to the plate.

Neither stepparents nor biological parents should ever be

expected to function in an isolated vacuum. The ideal situation is a working alliance between the parent and stepparent that will help to clarify the stepparent's role. Smart stepparenting depends on planning and strategic co-parenting.

Although planning is important, so is flexibility. One of the necessities in blending a stepfamily is for the parents and stepparents (on both sides of the equation, if this applies) to hold loosely to the visitation or custody schedule. With so many different schedules to accommodate, scheduling can become a difficult balancing act. It is his weekend, but she has a special mother-daughter event and wants to switch. It is her year to have the kids for Christmas, but this is the only year her ex-husband's grandparents will be around, so he wants to negotiate a change. With so many variables, it becomes virtually impossible to plan on anything you plan. Although it can be tempting for parents to try to rigidly enforce the custody schedule, wanting to avoid a missed opportunity to spend time with their children, allowing flexibility to accommodate unavoidable scheduling conflicts is the right thing to do.

It is essential for couples to continually strive to focus on what's best for the children, not just for themselves. That may entail putting aside frustration with the former spouse or other external factors and homing in on what will result in the least amount of stress and anxiety for the children. Parents must accept that they will most likely not see their children every day—that can be a tough pill to swallow, but it is often part of the prescription for divorce when kids are involved. If you operate and make decisions out of humility and empathy and allow the children time to adjust to their new lifestyle, you as a family will likely experience more blending and fewer areas of separation.

HOW IT SHOULD BE

I recently read an article about a blended family who had done something right. In typical fashion, a couple had married, had children, and then divorced. The story didn't disclose how many children they had, but they did have a daughter who was now twenty-one and had recently wed. There was no mention, either, of how long the couple had been divorced or how long it had been since the wife had remarried, but both the girl's stepdad and her biological dad were important to her.

Apparently the road for this blended family had not been smooth in the past when it came to getting along. This isn't surprising, because blending two families invariably requires a good deal of patience, forgiveness, and above all, humility. (That is why I fight so hard to help people stay married for life!) What brought this story into the limelight for me was a gesture made by the daughter's biological dad during her wedding ceremony. As he prepared to walk her down the aisle, he suddenly left her side and grabbed the hand of her stepdad, informing him through this spontaneous gesture that he should be a part of the ritual of giving her away.

A photographer memorably captured the emotion of the stepdad after he was asked to participate. The article quoted him saying how badly it had hurt him to be dressed in a tux without being a participant. The picture went viral. The bride's dad conceded to the stepdad that he had just as big a part in raising his child as he himself had. While the bride had dreamed of something like this happening, she had never thought it would be possible based on the family's history of strife.

The bride's dad made a statement about divorced couples that I think is worth repeating: "It's a shame more parents can't set aside their egos for an event like this. Kids should not have boundaries about who they love and who they care for. Unfortunately, many parents, through their arguing and bickering, want to keep kids closed in."[1]

Couples who have children and then divorce need to approach their new family dynamics by putting their children first. The visitation schedule, if it is an inconvenience to anyone, should inconvenience the child the least. I know of one couple who did their best to make life easier for the children: they deliberately arranged to live close to each other in an effort to eliminate some of the frustrations that invariably occur for children forced to adjust to living in two households. Keeping clothes at each parent's house eliminates the need for a suitcase or for making the child feel like a visitor. When parents live in close proximity to each other, the kids can maintain the friendships that existed before the divorce. I have known of couples who went so far as to keep their kids in the same houses, themselves moving in and out each week. Incorporating these kinds of tools won't entirely eliminate the challenges, but it will make the situation a little easier on the children. Other concessions might include the two families sitting together at sporting events and the biological and/or stepparents attending parent-teacher conferences together. One couple I know arranged twice, in conjunction with their new spouses, to spend family vacations together. I am not suggesting that the adults spent every moment as a foursome, but they did manage to foster unity for the sake of the children. It took all the adult players in that situation a few years to develop that kind of camaraderie, and it wouldn't have happened had God's hand not been in it.

HER STORY

After seven years of marriage and two children, Jenny called it quits. She wasn't happy and didn't think God wanted her unhappy. She wasn't a Christian at that time, so instead of running to God for answers, she gravitated to friends and others who would support her opinions. She did grow up with a faith of sorts, but it felt more like a faith in religion than a faith in God or the personal walk with Jesus she now experiences. She proceeded with the divorce, believing it was the right decision for her.

But had she been a Christian during her first marriage and understood how powerful God and prayer really are, she conceded that she would have stayed in her marriage, praying for her heart to be changed. But despite her decision and because of God's amazing grace, she was blessed to marry again, and together she and her new husband became Christians. As she explained to me, it was through prayer that they learned to better manage their stepfamily. It wasn't always easy, but with God's help they survived. She and her ex-husband lived only a few blocks from each other, which was great for the kids. But she frequently found it necessary to drive past his house on the way to somewhere or other and at times found it painful to see her kids playing outside there. It rankled her, as well, to notice new landscaping being installed at his house when he still owed her money.

She understood that all of this was tied in to the natural consequences of her decision to divorce, and her new husband would continually remind her that "It's just stuff" or "It's just money. It isn't worth the battle." She remembers how often God helped her hold her tongue when she had wanted to speak her mind, acknowledging after the fact that this would have done nothing to help the situation and would only have bred more contempt instead of compassion. While she didn't allow her former husband to take advantage of her, she learned to refrain from commenting about every seemingly unfair transaction that occurred—and certainly to avoid talking about any of this in front of the children.

She realized that, shortly after her divorce, she had considered it to be her ex-husband's *privilege* (as opposed to right) to spend time with the children, but now she accepted that he was as entitled to time with them as she was. Just because she was doing the majority of the work involving the kids and their activities didn't mean his rights were diminished. This is an all-too-common battle waged even by people who stay married. In retrospect, she acknowledges that navigating the maze of stepfamily life has helped her understand God's truth about dying to self.

TRUTH

[Jesus] said to them all: "If anyone desires to come after Me, let him deny himself, and take up his cross daily, and follow Me. For whoever desires to save his life will lose it, but whoever loses his life for My sake will save it."
LUKE 9:23–24 NKJV

GUARD YOUR TONGUE

One of the keys for successfully managing a blended family is being careful to guard our tongue. Just because we want to say something doesn't mean we should. In Proverbs 21:23 Solomon reminds us that "those who guard their mouths and their tongues keep themselves from calamity." This is certainly true in the context of speaking about your former spouse in the presence of your children. While there may be times when it is necessary to share a truth with your children about their mom or dad in the interest of their safety or well-being, too often a frustrated ex-spouse is merely venting about her or his former spouse's behavior—not something the children need to hear.

When you talk about your former spouse in an offensive

way, your children, who rightly view themselves as being 50 percent of that parent, may well take your criticism personally, as though you are somehow implicating them. They will probably not receive the critique in the same spirit as an objective adult or friend would who might be able to empathize with you. In God's eyes, this kind of venting equates to judging. It may not feel like that to you; you are, after all, referring to your ex-husband or ex-wife, with whom the kids know you don't see eye to eye, but God views it that way. We aren't entitled as Christians to speak disparagingly about anyone else just because that person has hurt us or we were once married to her or him. This is still making a judgment—a right God reserves for Himself!

TRUTH

"Do not judge, or you too will be judged. For in the same way you judge others, you will be judged, and with the measure you use, it will be measured to you."
MATTHEW 7:1–2

Equally imperative is that we not force our children to function as messengers or go-betweens when it comes to ourselves and our previous marriage partners. If you are still angry at your ex-spouse, figure out a way to let go of your resentment to the degree that you can talk with her or him directly. This is part of being an adult—a role you have no business foisting on your children in this situation. Children take in more than we realize, and they can sense tension between their parents as easily as a bear sniffs out honey. You can't fool them, and when they have spent the weekend with their other parent and you casually ask them questions about what they did and who was there, don't fool yourself into thinking they won't figure out that you are snooping. Even if you aren't, it will be hard for you to prove your intentions. There are undoubtedly some cases in which a parent has legitimate concerns about what is happening at her or his former spouse's house but may have to resort to legal measures to find out the truth, rather than attempting to cast their child in the role of spy or informant.

The at times complicated back-and-forth behavioral dance on the part of ex-spouses boils down on both sides to ego and pride. Regardless of the shape or circumstances of your family, if the two of you as parents can no longer live together, at the very least you had better resolve, for the sake of your children, to look beyond your egos.

NONCOMPETE CLAUSE

Many individuals in the field of sales are requested to sign a "noncompete clause" upon their hire into a company. The idea is that if that salesperson ever decides to leave the company and go to work for the competition, they are prohibited from bringing their current customers with them. While there are undoubtedly ways around this clause, the intent is for people to be fair and honest.

In my opinion, it might be beneficial for couples with

children who divorce to sign a "no compete clause." I say this based on a tendency I have observed for one parent to outshine the other in an attempt to win over the loyalty of the children or lure them away from the other parent. This is a sad reality to acknowledge, but it does happen. Whether based on guilt or pride, parents have been known to pile on the material goods or load up the pockets of their offspring with money in an attempt to ensure their loyalty. While legitimate circumstances may be factors here (perhaps one parent handles finances better or can afford more than the other), this different ability or approach doesn't have to be flaunted or used manipulatively.

The best way to determine whether you are engaging in this kind of behavior is to check your heart. What was the motivation behind your buying that new bike when the one your daughter has been riding had a few good years left? Was that extra twenty dollars you slipped into her pocket based on necessity, or did you feel the need for some accolades from your child? In 1 Samuel 16:7 God instructs Samuel in his quest to determine God's choice among Jesse's sons for Israel's kingship, "Do not consider his appearance or his height, for I have rejected him. The LORD does not look at the things people look at. People look at the outward appearance, but the LORD looks at the heart." You may be able to fool some people, but God always knows your heart.

Instead of provoking competition with your former spouse, try to stir up within yourself some compassion and empathy. Try to look at your attempts to win affection from his or her point of view. Imagine how you would feel if you were in your ex-spouse's shoes. Because of unwise decisions, a former spouse sometimes finds herself or himself in a less-than-desirable position, but just as God extends His grace to all of us despite our poor choices, we owe it to Him and others to pass along that grace. If parents or step-parents are competing, it should be for a healthy balance of time and effort directed toward successfully raising their mutual children.

IT ISN'T GREENER ON THE OTHER SIDE

If you as a parent reading this are still married to your child(ren)'s other parent, I hope you will read this chapter as a reminder from the other side of the issue that divorce and managing a stepfamily is never easy. I recognize that there may be days when your marriage is at a low point, to the extent that you may wonder at least momentarily whether you should stay in your union; if you find yourself in that position, read this chapter again, approaching it as a reminder that the grass isn't always greener on the other side and that you might just need to fertilize your own a little more. I suspect that many, if not most, couples managing a blended family situation could attest to at least a degree of truth in that statement.

The woman whose story I told earlier truly imagined that she and her former husband would be good friends from the onset of the divorce and that his family would continue to embrace her. Sadly, this expectation was an imaginative flight. She simply failed to take into account the degree of hurt everyone involved would experience, from in-laws to members of her own extended family. She reluctantly admitted in retrospect that she had been focused solely on her own unhappiness and her desperate desire to change the situation. While the outcome was ultimately positive, she attributes this to her new relationship with Christ and her ability to learn from His truth and grace and apply that insight to the circumstances of her blended family. Still, she is adamant in encouraging others to remain in their marriages, recognizing that those same godly principles can be applied to staying married for life.

TRUTH IN THE WORD

The material in this chapter may feel harsh in some respects, but I have come by my conclusions honestly, based on seeing so many families torn apart by divorce and witnessing so many children caught in the crossfire. I have a desperate desire to see stepfamilies thrive by continuing to parent God's way, and I believe that can happen by applying the simple but profound truths God has spelled out in His Word for all of us involved in relationships. It is vital for each of us, too, to receive and accept His gift of grace. I am painfully aware that many people who have gone through a divorce live with a tremendous amount of guilt and shame. The sense of failure they feel as a spouse and parent can sometimes be the catalyst driving poor decisions and behavior in their stepfamily settings.

The author of Hebrews directs his readers in Hebrews 12:15 to "see to it that no one falls short of the grace of God and that no bitter root grows up to cause trouble and defile many." If we refuse to receive the grace God so freely offers, we will become consumed by guilt and condemnation without our even realizing it, to the point that our actions will come to reflect the pent-up frustration that is more often about ourselves than about anyone else. God understands that if we decline to accept His grace or forgiveness, or if we refuse to forgive others, we will carry bitterness in our hearts that will spread like a virus into every area of our lives.

Parents who have divorced and are trying to stepparent may be harboring feelings of self-condemnation and guilt, hampering their ability to model their parenting after the attitudes and behavior patterns exemplified by Jesus. As God reminds us in Romans 8:1, "There is now no condemnation for those who are in Christ Jesus." If we sense condemnation, it is because we are choosing not to accept the forgiveness and grace God offers in response to our repentance.

I encourage you to examine your heart to see whether you have any need to repent. Once you have taken this step, you will find yourself free to accept God's forgiveness and receive His grace—the foundation for helping your family blend and win more often at home.

QUESTIONS TO CONSIDER

1. The keys to managing a blended family are communication, flexibility, and respect.

   How could you improve in the area of flexibility when it comes to the custody schedule and putting your children's needs ahead of your own?

   Identify some specific ways in which you could improve the communication between yourself and your former spouse.

2. It is imperative to avoid making your children messengers or go-betweens between yourself and their other parent.

   If you have been expecting your children to take on this role, what can you change?

3. Instead of creating competition with your former spouse, seek to create within yourself some compassion and empathy.

   In what ways might you be competing with your former spouse, and how can you replace that behavior with compassion and empathy?

4. Many people who have divorced feel a tremendous amount of guilt and shame.

   In what areas of your life do you feel guilt and shame, either with regard to your divorce or to some other circumstance, and what steps can you take to help remedy that situation?

   _____

   ## DAN'S REALITY CHECK

   We all struggle with guilt and shame that stem from pride, and we allow them to infiltrate our relationships. This struggle will continue until the day we return to our heavenly Father in that place where there will be no more tears. Until that time, we need to immerse ourselves in God's Word, believe His promises, and surrender our ego-driven pride daily so we can live with more humility.

   _____

CHAPTER 7

The Truth about the Roles of Mom and Dad

Let's face it: the role of mom or dad isn't easy. Each comes with its own set of challenges—and its unique and precious victories. I have a suspicion that if you asked most any mom to compare her parenting role to her husband's in terms of difficulty, she'd express it as being a little more concentrated and a little bit harder. I am also pretty sure that if you asked most dads, they would be inclined to agree. In truth, though, the roles shouldn't be considered harder or easier but simply different.

God designed men and women to complement each other's strengths and weaknesses. Yet while men and women are equal in God's sight in terms of their intrinsic value, their gifts and abilities aren't necessarily equal or even directly comparable. One thing we know for sure: God intended it to be just that way for the benefit of children.

GUARDING YOUR TREASURE

I grew up in the little town of Six Mile, South Carolina. During the time I lived there and for years thereafter, my dad accumulated a tremendous amount of—dare I say it?—junk. It is amazing to see. I had tried to describe his treasure trove to my friends, but in this case seeing was believing. One time I brought two of my friends to my childhood home for a firsthand peek into the barn housing my dad's "riches." They were blown away at the amount he had stowed.

One time when my father was rummaging around in his barn, he accidentally caught his foot on a cable, causing him to fall. Unable to disentangle himself or get to his feet, he literally screamed for about ten minutes before a neighbor finally heard and came to his rescue. He was thankfully unscathed, but the incident provided for me a good illustration of how easily we men can get caught up in the very things that threaten to distract us from what should be our priorities—like fatherhood. The issue might be hobbies, outside interests, or a steady stream of work-related e-mails during our evenings or weekends. When our life is full of junk, it is easy to get tripped up by things that aren't where they belong.

It would be hard to deny that negotiating the demands—and delights—of life constitutes a balancing act. For example, while there may indeed be times when our jobs necessitate working additional hours outside our normal routine, when work becomes our priority to the point that our wives and family get relegated to a secondary status, we have gotten ourselves into a situation. One that can cause a dad—even the best one—to take a tumble. It isn't just work that can make a man stumble either; it can just as well be sports, a collection of classic automobiles or vintage whatever, hunting, or even training for a running event. If we are filling up our lives with so much activity that it is preventing us from investing in the lives of our children, it is time for a junk dump. If this sounds like a problem for you, take a good, hard look at your schedule and determine what you can rearrange or eliminate to free up more space for your family.

I understand and appreciate that a lot of men work hard all week long and would benefit from some rest and rejuvenation over the weekends. Yet no matter how overburdened we may feel—or be—it is vitally important for us to negotiate a balance between much-needed rest and time with our families. Is it necessary to watch football all afternoon on Sunday, or could we be content with one game? Is there a way to incorporate our children into whatever it is we need to get done around the house? Kids love getting attention from their parents, even when it means doing yard work or cleaning out the garage—not to mention the invaluable learning that takes place in that context.

Get rid of the junk in your life so you can make room for the treasure—your family!

CALLED TO LEADERSHIP

Although parental roles have changed drastically within recent decades, with many family scenarios no longer following traditional paradigms, readers familiar with scripture will agree that God has endowed fathers, as heads of their households, with the privilege of and primary responsibility for leading and providing for their children—a reality we as believing men may take too lightly. I can't tell you how often I see women alone in church with their children. When I ask the wife where Dad is, the reply is too often that though her husband doesn't go to church, he supports everyone else's attendance. Does that sound familiar?

On that day when we stand before our King to give an account of our lives, we men will be held accountable for our performance in that God-assigned leadership role. Even if we are going through the "right" motions, looking the part of a promise-keeping dad just isn't good enough. God expects our actions and attitudes to grow out of and demonstrate our inner reality—to model what God expects from us not only in our *doing* but more essentially in our *being*. Let's never forget while we are at it that our primary audience is our children—and that they are a discriminating bunch, the hardest of all to fool.

God created people in His image, and just as God is our heavenly Father, He intended for earthly dads to function as an imitation of Himself to their children. We men don't have to look too far to find the template God has designed for us to follow. It is spelled out in His Word.

> *These commandments that I give you today are to be on your hearts. Impress them on your children. Talk about them when you sit at home and when you walk along the road, when you lie down and when you get up. Tie them as symbols on your hands and bind them on your foreheads. Write them on the doorframes of your houses and on your gates.*
> DEUTERONOMY 6:6–9

God couldn't have been clearer than He was in Deuteronomy 6 about the need for fathers to function as spiritual leaders for their children, communicating God's commands and expectations to them. This kind of instruction doesn't

necessarily—or even optimally—take place in a formal setting. Talk to your children when you are playing with them,
when your "captive" audience is enjoying a road trip with you
behind the wheel, or when you are driving to or from school
or some extracurricular activity and the opportunity presents itself. Whenever a situation arises that might connect
with one of God's commandments, make that connection
clear. Don't wait for a family devotional setting (good for
you, though, if you do oversee devotions!) to bring up something that is in the Bible. Make conversations about God as
normal and as regular as brushing teeth. Teach your children
that walking with the Lord is a daily effort, not a once-a-
week ritual when everybody gets dressed up, piles into the
car, and does their best to behave for a couple of hours.
Gathering regularly with the body of Christ and serving the
church and others in His name certainly is important, but
your children can grow and benefit from so much that can
be said and done at home or in the car. How much more
instructive for you as a dad to integrate your faith in terms of
your family life than to compartmentalize it!

The Deuteronomy 6 passage also reveals that it is *our*
responsibility as dads—not the church's or the Christian
school's or the youth pastor's—to teach our kids about God
and about life. That isn't to suggest that other people can't or
won't positively influence our children. We should pray for
that to happen, but that kind of reinforcement should complement whatever we are teaching at home—a between-meal
pick-me-up, as opposed to the only spiritual sustenance

our children receive. Fathers, of course, aren't the only ones responsible for this teaching; mothers play a major role in Christian education as well. Still, it is the fathers who should be leading the way. The Bible makes it clear that *they have been given primary accountability* to God to make sure that training in godliness happens in the home.

TRUTH

"For I have chosen him, so that he will direct his children and his household after him to keep the way of the LORD by doing what is right and just, so that the LORD will bring about for Abraham what he has promised him."
GENESIS 18:19

Listen, my son, to your father's instruction and do not forsake your mother's teaching.
PROVERBS 1:8

THE STATISTICS SPEAK LOUDLY

If you don't believe fathers have tremendous influence over children, consider the following statistics:

- Children in father-absent homes are almost four times more likely to be poor. In 2011, 12 percent of children in married-couple families were living in poverty, compared to 44 percent of children in mother-only families.[1]

- Even after controlling for community context, there is significantly more drug use among children who do not live with their mother and father.[2]
- A study of 263 thirteen- to eighteen-year-old unmarried adolescent women seeking psychological services found that the adolescents from father-absent homes were 3.5 times more likely to experience pregnancy than were adolescents from father-present homes. Moreover, the rate of pregnancy among adolescents from father-absent homes was 17.4 percent, compared to a 4 percent rate in the general adolescent population.[3]
- Individuals from father-absent homes were found to be 279 percent more likely to carry guns and deal drugs than peers living with their fathers.[4]
- In 2012, 57.6 percent of black children, 31.2 percent of Hispanic children, and 20.7 percent of white children were living in the absence of their biological fathers.[5]
- In 1992, of all youths sitting in prisons, 85 percent grew up in a fatherless home.[6]
- Children of single-parent homes are more than twice as likely to commit suicide.[7]

It is hard to argue with statistics. It seems safe to conclude, at the very least, that a father plays a significant role in family life.

The bond between a father and a daughter is critical in terms of her degree of success. Dr. Margaret J. Meeker, a pediatrician with more than twenty years of experience counseling girls, authored a book titled *Strong Fathers, Strong Daughters: 10 Secrets Every Father Should Know*, in which she lists some findings from her research on the influence of fathers. Here are a few:

- Daughters whose fathers provide warmth and control achieve higher rates of academic success. Girls involved with their dads are twice as likely to stay in school.
- Daughters who are close to their fathers exhibit a lower incidence of anxiety and withdrawal behaviors.
- The likelihood that daughters will engage in premarital sex, drug use, or alcohol plummets when their dads are involved in their lives.
- Daughters who feel their fathers care about them and who feel connected with their dads have significantly fewer suicide attempts and exhibit fewer instances of body dissatisfaction, depression, low self-esteem, substance abuse, and unhealthy weight.
- A daughter's self-esteem is best predicted by her father's loving affection.[8]

Meeker points out that "from the first years of a girl's life her father is larger than life. She looks up to him, and for the rest of her life she craves his admiration, his respect and his affection."[9] On this basis, my organization, Winning At Home, hosts an annual winter ball for fathers and daughters. The idea is not only to offer an opportunity for fathers to spend quality time with their little girls but to show their daughters how a man should respect and treat women. At the event, we offer activities that encourage dads and daughters to talk, and we structure the evening in such a way that dads don't end up talking to other dads while their daughters run around the room. After talking about the power of prayer, we give dads a few moments to pray over their daughters, teaching again the importance of inviting Christ into that relationship. The evening is designed to be fun but is purposeful as well. It began as a one-night annual event but grew in popularity to the extent that we now offer two evenings each year—evidence of a hunger for opportunities to come together as fathers and daughters.

---

*A daughter needs a dad to be the
standard against which she will judge all men.*
UNKNOWN

In Ephesians 6 God is abundantly clear, through Paul, about the father's role with his children. In verse 4 Paul addresses dads in attention-grabbing terms: "Fathers, do not exasperate your children; instead, bring them up in the training and instruction of the Lord." God doesn't presume that fathers will never become annoyed or frustrated with their children; what He does expect is that, in lieu of an emotionally charged reaction implied in the form of arbitrary, man-made commands, which will exasperate them, the Christian father will respond rationally and lovingly, based on scriptural principles. God's words in the Bible constitute our secret weapon as Christian fathers. We have the guidance of the Holy Spirit and God's Word at our disposal as we help our children grow into the adults God intends them to be. With God in our corner, we have no need to rely upon our own impulses, ideas, or wisdom.

FOUR WISHES FOR MY CHILDREN

When my children were small and I envisioned what life might be like for them someday, I hoped certain experiences wouldn't pass them by. Not to sound sadistic, but there were key mile markers, negative in themselves, that I hated to think any of them might miss:

I hoped that someday they would have a job they couldn't stand.

I hoped that someone they loved would let them down.

I hoped that somehow they would experience physical pain.

I hoped that something toward which they would devote their best effort would fall flat.

Jobs are important, I know, and income is necessary. Still, I didn't want my kids to put too much stock in what they were doing for a living. That is why, for at least a little while, I hoped they would work like crazy someplace with little payback in terms of money or recognition.

A job like that, I realized, would develop humility in them. They would come to understand that work isn't everything—and that earning money isn't necessarily enjoyable in itself. They would identify at least for a time with the bottom of the working-class totem pole, and hopefully this would teach them to care about people.

I wanted—and still want—my kids to know love—to experience it to its fullest, most complicated depths. But I wanted them to understand that love doesn't get handed out as often or as fairly as it should and that it doesn't always come easily.

I also wanted them to learn that love is sturdy enough to survive disappointment. I hoped my kids would get their hearts broken a bit by people about whom they cared deeply. I hoped this would help them appreciate that devotion is powerful and delicate. I hoped they would be softer and more resilient as a result.

This sounds ridiculous, I know—and it *is* a little ridiculous: still today it kills me to sit on the sidelines as my kids go through trials and sadness. It is heart-wrenching to see them hurting. Still, I have become convinced that they are better for it in the end.

It is amazing, though, to come to recognize that they can

indeed endure and overcome, and it is even more amazing to see the quality individuals who emerge as a result. When it is all said and done, the hurt is never for nothing.

I hesitate to say it, but still today I hope my kids will have to experience some physical pain. I hope they will fall down, get sick, or sprain something. I hope it will hurt enough to make them remember, to make them extra grateful for muscles and bones that are in working order.

I hope it makes them stop and feel for a while, that it gives them compassion for the student in the wheelchair, the grandparent in the nursing home, and the friend with cancer. For the sake of my own nerves, I hope the hurt is just for a while and just a little, but for the sake of their long-term well-being, I hope that someday each of my kids may know what it is like to be unwell.

And still today I hope they will fail at something. I hope that at least once their best may result in a complete flop. I hope the letdown is a hard lesson, but I hope they learn it well. I hope it teaches them about their weaknesses, but mostly that it compels them to press on even harder the next time.

You see, I want the best for my children. I want them to be people of character and integrity and strength, and those aren't qualities that just pop up out of nowhere. They are picked up over time, by walking through muck and mire.

Even though it is awful for me to sit back and watch, sometimes I have to do just that. Throughout their lives, I will continue to watch my grown kids endure struggles and hardship and grief, and I will do nothing but encourage them to press on.

I will stand at the end and cheer, ready to leap when it is over—to celebrate them for learning, loving, feeling, and persevering.

THE ROLE OF MOTHER

Motherhood is grueling. I have arrived at this conclusion not only by talking to many moms but by witnessing my own wife in her role as mother. Being a mom to children under five can be especially draining. I remember vividly my experiences with changing diapers, chasing after little ones when something breakable was within their reach, and wiping more runny noses than I care to count. It is flat-out demanding, even when two parents are functioning well as a team.

Moms bear a heavy load when it comes to caring for little ones. Even for a guy like me, who came alongside his wife in sharing the parenting duties, I suspect that many small tasks would never have been accomplished had it not been for her. If she hadn't filled in the gaps, I can't help but imagine my adult children might still be crammed into toddler-sized clothing and eating with their fingers.

An at-home mom rarely leaves the environment in which she works—with the result that uncompleted tasks are staring her down at every turn. She never really knows when to call it *a day*. The same is true for moms who work outside the home. They end their day at the office and then come home and transform into the energetic mommy. In either case, the demands are relentless. Even when they go to sleep at night, those vigilant moms do so knowing they may have a middle-of-the-night interruption because someone needs a glass of water or has an upset tummy.

I think moms are remarkable for many reasons, although unfortunately not everyone at every point will agree or appreciate this designation. Just ask an adolescent boy who is frustrated by a nagging mom who insists he wear a coat, or ask a teen girl who doesn't appreciate Mom's protective nature when defining what is an appropriate school wardrobe. Not every moment will be picture-perfect, but the overall effect of Mom's love and care will eventually dawn on most kids, to the point that with a little added maturity they will even come to recognize and appreciate her consistent contributions as foundational for their lives. And while the scriptures may primarily address fathers in this area, it goes without saying that it is also the mother's role not only to help spiritually guide the children but to uphold and model in her own behavior the principles for godly living laid out in the Word.

TRUTH

He tends his flock like a shepherd: He gathers the lambs in his arms and carries them close to his heart; he gently leads those that have young.
ISAIAH 40:11

MOMS ARE LIKE SUPERHEROES!

Although all moms are different, they do have some traits in common, and some people consider them to be superheroes in disguise for the way they nurture and care for their children. In true mom fashion, they fly into action when the occasion calls for it. They will leap tall buildings in a single bound to reach their child in need, fly faster than a speeding bullet when their baby calls out their name in the middle of the night, and can be more powerful than a locomotive when their child has been wronged. And while kryptonite puts Superman in jeopardy, when it comes to family dynamics, anyone daring to come between a mom and her little one may be considered a threat.

Yet while moms may manifest the personality and power of a superhero when it comes to the interests of their kids, they are not always recognized or appreciated for their efforts. The funny thing is that the very criterion that makes them so special is that they do whatever is needed in the full awareness that they will receive no recognition. And they do it with excellence. They understand that being underappreciated or not applauded is part of the gig. That doesn't mean they always like that part, but they know deep down that their children love them fiercely, whether or not they are willing to reveal that secret.

Being a mother is learning about strengths you didn't know
you had and dealing with fears you didn't know existed.
LINDA WOOTEN

The website Finding Joy compiled a list of twenty-four awe-some things moms do, and I wanted to share a few of them with you in recognition of the strength of moms:

> They will cook meals, slave over meals, and invent meals despite the fact that they will invariably hear someone say they don't like it or receive no comment one way or the other.
>
> They are willing to give up a lot of sleep and will stay awake at night until all of their chicks are safe inside the coop.
>
> They have an amazing ability to find anything that is lost. Even when a child claims they have looked everywhere for that special item, a mom can spot it near-instantaneously.
>
> They understand that doors slammed or words hurled in anger are normal kids' stuff, even though it hurts to hear. Moms have feelings too, but they just keep going, apparently unruffled. Another hidden talent.
>
> They can translate two-year-old speak. They have been given a special ear to understand the early verbal ventures of their children even when nobody else can.
>
> They are skilled diplomats who walk that fine line between negotiation and bribery. Moms use this skill when inappropriate behavior shows up in public. They bring it out when children find it

difficult to sleep or when they just can't reach an agreement on what movie to watch.

They also believe in their kids and their dreams. Nobody will ever love, champion, and support us like our mom.[10]

TRUTH

She watches over the affairs of her household and does not eat the bread of idleness. Her children arise and call her blessed; her husband also, and he praises her: "Many women do noble things, but you surpass them all." Charm is deceptive, and beauty is fleeting; but a woman who fears the LORD is to be praised. Honor her for all that her hands have done, and let her works bring her praise at the city gate.

PROVERBS 31:27–31

RESPONSIBLE AS BOTH MOM AND DAD

An organization where I live pairs adult mentors with at-risk children to provide them guidance in a variety of areas. A friend of mine is a mentor in this program, and he shared with me recently that a small child he is mentoring was not getting much sleep at night. Apparently this little boy would force himself to stay up late so he could see his mom before he went to sleep. His mom works two shifts and usually comes home after he has gone to bed. This poignant story got me thinking about the many children around the world who love and desperately want to be with frequently absent parents.

We often think that kids don't want to be around their parents, especially as they get older, but more often than not kids crave the security of having them near. In the case of a single-parent family, that statement is probably even more accurate.

If you are parenting in conjunction with a partner, close your eyes for a moment and try to imagine what it would be like to do it all on your own. Making lunches, cleaning clothes, driving and picking up before and after every activity, helping with homework, grocery shopping, and most likely working full-time to pay all the bills. The sole responsibility for everything falls on your shoulders. If you can catch even a mental glimpse of how that might feel, you may want to consider coming alongside one person representing this group of hardworking individuals.

According to the US Census, in 2007 there were 13.7 million single parents who were together responsible for raising 21.8 million children.[11] That is approximately 26 percent of all children in the country under the age of twenty-one. In talking with single parents over the years, I have learned that one of the biggest frustrations they deal with has to do with assumptions people make about their lifestyle. Many find themselves embarrassed or angry when asked whether their children all have the same dad. Another false assumption is that the children of single parents are destined to do poorly in school. Some have expressed frustration that their bosses fail to understand when they need time off for the kids. Many single parents have no one else to care for their sick children or to take them to appointments.

To complicate the situation still further, many single parents work two jobs to make ends meet—while still taking very seriously their responsibility for their children's care. You could probably identify a few such families from your neighborhood, school, or church. Pause for a moment to consider what you could do to lighten someone's load. Could you help her get some laundry done? Pick up a few items for her from the grocery store?

If you think your role as mother or father is hard, imagine having to take on both roles. Then imagine that you aren't wired to be the nurturing type but your child is hurting and needs a hug and some tender encouragement. Or that you have no reserve left after disciplining your children to muster the energy to play with them.

I count hardworking single parents among my everyday heroes. Many are not in that position by choice, but regardless of how they arrived there, the situation is incredibly challenging. As followers of Christ we—men and women alike—are called to "parent" the fatherless and defend the widow or otherwise unattached adult who finds herself cast in a parenting role. I firmly believe God wants us to rally around single parents and try to help them out in any way we can.

TRUTH

A father to the fatherless, a defender to widows,
is God in his holy dwelling.
PSALM 68:5

THE ROLE OF PARENTS—IT ISN'T FOR COWARDS!

As I listened recently to a mom sharing an incidence of her child talking back to her, repeatedly telling her she hated her, and defying her every instruction, the thought occurred to me that parenting is not for cowards. As I am out and about, I naturally tend to observe the interactions among family members. There's the child who throws a temper tantrum in the middle of the frozen food aisle. Or the one who is told to take a time-out but proceeds to stand his ground and stare at the parent without moving a centimeter. Or the teen who brazenly and continually rolls his eyes, texts while you are talking to him, or talks back to you in a disrespectful way. Parenting is not for cowards.

Too often we see people who lack the maturity to understand what parenting even means. For several decades our society has dealt with an onslaught of young girls who are—ready or not!—finding themselves young moms and young men who are becoming young fathers. Insecure, uninitiated, baffled, and overwhelmed kids themselves, they lack the resources to begin to grasp the responsibility and hard work it takes to parent. Biologically equipped but otherwise totally unprepared young people need to understand that every sexual encounter can lead to a pregnancy, even when protection is in place. Just ask the husband who has had a vasectomy and then gotten his wife pregnant. There are no guarantees!

When a couple thinks about having a child, they conjure up images of babies and sweetness. That is only natural—and it is the fun part. Despite the inevitable demands, parenting is relatively comfortable when your child is asleep periodically for two to three hours at a stretch. Even though your newborn knows how to "talk back" to you by crying, he can't yet mouth the words that will cut to the core. Then when he morphs into a toddler, he begins to show signs of some tartness to his disposition. He still says the cutest things, but there comes a day when you need to be strong because his sweetness starts to sour like milk that is past its expiration date. It doesn't taste good, and you are left to wonder who switched out your sweet baby.

Parenting is for people who are disciplined and well-balanced, who know how to take charge of life. Since you are reading this in the first place, you are probably at a point of assessing, "Well, that's not me." And putting the "shoe" on my own foot, I will have to concede that I totally agree. There are days when I feel disengaged, don't want to be responsible, or would rather not deal with those inevitable family situations that still arise after the kids are grown and on their own. But that is not an option. That is why we can't be cowardly.

Don't worry that children never listen to you;
worry that they are always watching you.
ROBERT FULGHUM

Being a good parent means confronting and facing issues that are sometimes embarrassing or even humiliating. That goes with the territory. It also involves engaging in tough conversations—some of which are our responsibility to initiate. If we are predisposed to shy away from confrontation, the results won't be positive.

That is why I am pointing out that parenting isn't for cowards. Even at its best, the role is challenging and the demands are high. The good parents are viewed in retrospect as having been instrumental in shaping the lives of their children. They were willing to take on that responsibility even though it all too frequently required toughness in relation to their children.

My challenge to you: Don't be a coward. Be a comrade. Be involved in the lives of your children, and I can guarantee you will win more often at home.

TRUTH IN THE WORD

We don't have to do this parenting thing alone. God has provided His Word as a guide. We simply have to adhere to it. In 2 Timothy 3:16–17, Paul reminds us that "all Scripture is God-breathed and is useful for teaching, rebuking, correcting and training in righteousness, so that the servant of God may be thoroughly equipped for every good work." Our job as parents is to raise our children to be servants of God and to do everything we can to thoroughly equip them for every good work. That may sound like a tall order, but God has given us explicit instructions throughout the Bible.

We sometimes get confused and think our job as parents is to raise an Olympic athlete, a scholar, or perhaps the next president of the United States. When we think in those terms, we are putting more focus on what our children are going to do in life than on who they will become. If our emphasis is more on the character of our children, on training them how to serve God, His will for their life will naturally evolve. If we lead from God's perspective and lean into His Word (a comforting picture, isn't it?) for guidance and direction, parenting will be less worrisome!

We make the job unnecessarily complicated when we try to do it on our own. When we as parents fixate on goals and accomplishments instead of training our gaze on Jesus as our relational model for parenting, we struggle more often. As Paul calls us in Romans 12:2, "Do not conform to the pattern of this world, but be transformed by the renewing of your mind. Then you will be able to test and approve what God's will is—his good, pleasing and perfect will."

QUESTIONS TO CONSIDER

1. Get rid of the clutter in your life so you can make room for the real treasure—your family!

   What junk in your life may be preventing you from making time for your family?

2. God created people in His image, and just as He is our heavenly Father, He intended for earthly dads to function as a replica of Himself in relation to their children.

   In what ways do you replicate God to your children?

3. While scripture may primarily address fathers in this area, the mother, too, has a vital role in helping to spiritually guide the children and to uphold and model the principles stated in the Word.

   How are you using scripture to speak into the lives of your children?

4. God wants us to rally around single parents and to try to help them out whenever we can.

   In what ways could you help out a single parent in your neighborhood or community? Be specific and intentional in your answer.

5. If we lead from God's perspective and lean into His Word for guidance and direction, parenting becomes less worrisome!

   How can you begin to lead more from God's perspective rather than your own?

   _____

   ## DAN'S REALITY CHECK

   Whether you are a father or a mother or have taken on both roles, make a conscious choice to respond to situations that arise from a biblical perspective. After all, it is your heartfelt desire for your children to be first and foremost servants of the King—not slaves to the world.

   _____

CHAPTER 8

The Truth about Preparing for A to Z but Living from A to B

Life is hard, and parenting another person's life is even harder. But if you have been blessed to be a parent, then you have been called by God to this privilege of helping to raise children to first and foremost become followers of Christ. Although our first inclination as parents is to raise our children for their future career, it is not what God calls us to. First, we are called to raise our children to seek and know the Lord. God's plan may be that He calls your children to a particular vocation, but your job is to make sure before that happens that they know the Lord.

That is the underlying truth of our responsibility as followers of Jesus Christ who become parents. That is a daunting task in and of itself. Add to that all of the other responsibilities that are required, such as feeding, clothing, nurturing, and housing them, and that amounts to a lot of pressure for parents to absorb.

But Christ is not only our Redeemer; He is our reliever! He can relieve all of that pressure if we will just follow His Word and His example. Christ *is* truth and grace, and we need His help to parent with truth and grace because we can't do it alone. God knew that when He designed the world and created the first parents, Adam and Eve. He knows everything. He sees the greater picture. He knows our needs before we do. He loves our children more than we do.

God knew my daughter Anna would leave us, but He also knew she would come back. As her parents, we didn't always believe that would happen. So while we brought our daughter Anna up to know the Lord, she ran from the things of God for a season. She chose to walk away. And that possibility exists for all of our children. Many of you have also raised children to know the Lord, and they have rebelled. That is their choice and not your fault. It will "feel" like your fault, and the enemy will try to convince you that their rebellion was because of your parenting or lack thereof, but rebellion was their decision. God also gave them free will. He only wants their love freely, not because their parents told them to love God. And when they return, it won't instantly be easy, nor will everything go back to normal. As I conclude this book, my wife and I are still dealing with the ramifications of when our daughter chose to leave our household.

Healing is a process. We can all celebrate when a child wants to return home, but the reality is there is a good amount of pain and hurt in her life and in our life that we must eventually confront. But not on her first day home. Our daughter sought professional counseling, which was very helpful. This counselor not only helped our daughter reconcile her decision, but she continued to give us guidance in terms of making sure we were patient as the healing process occurred. While a parent in this situation will probably deal with a combination of anger and blame, a child will put incredible blame on herself. She will feel like a failure. She will feel like she is no longer wanted. She will call herself the outcast of the family. She will put all kinds of monikers on her life and her name because she has a pile of guilt heaped on herself. For example, every time we would mention a story or something that happened in the past, we could see the pain in our daughter's eyes, and yet it was something that we needed to talk about. Healing is a process. For us, I know it is going to take years. One of the greatest lessons we learned is that a child must relearn to love herself. When a person has rebelled and gone against the way of God, she has essentially fallen out of love with who He made her to be, a child in His image. And the enemy is a master at using that to make her feel worthless. This makes the process of recovering and healing very slow and painful.

When a child has rebelled or has simply been disobedient in some way and parents are at a loss of what to do, God has the ability to write straight using crooked lines. In other words, God can do what we can't do. He can take evil and turn it for good. Even in the process of Anna coming home, I have had to go through some recovery myself. As parents, we need to realize that the Lord will use and redeem things that we consider lost. I remember once when my wife was sitting and crying, just thinking about our daughter and her future. She made the statement, "My dreams for my daughter are shattered." That is how the enemy wants us to think. Although my wife's statement may have been true, what is not true is that God's dreams for our daughter were shattered. I believe that Anna's greatest days are ahead because God is a redeemer and restorer. I believe the recovery for us as parents, regardless of the situations we are dealing with, will be tremendous when God is in the mix. But it will take some time. That brings me to my point of why we need to prepare for A to Z but live from A to B.

What I mean is that we live in the present but tend to parent in the future. We jump ahead of ourselves because we are so desperate to see how our children are going to "turn out." We focus on our own vision for their lives instead of God's vision. So while we need to be practical and prepare for the future, such as giving our children an education, planning financially so we can purchase a home, or any number of practical things we plan for on a daily basis, we need to live day by day or we will miss the entire journey.

For example, when Anna returned to us, our vision was for the recovery and healing to happen overnight. We focused on what we wanted the end result to be, which was for Anna to be walking confidently in the Lord and for all of us to be happy and getting along. Of course, God can and does do miracles that can bring about some changes overnight, but in reality that is not how He typically works. God wants us and our children to learn lessons throughout the restoration process, which we sometimes refer to as "the struggle." As I have heard people say or post on social media, that struggle is real. And that is how God intends it to be, because He knows that is where we will learn to be dependent on Him!

Grace will also triumph through this period. If we continue to show grace to our children, we will see tremendous restoration. There will be times in your parenting journey when showing grace to your child will seem counterintuitive, especially when she or he has hurt you deeply. A delicate balance must be maintained between truth and grace, but in most cases, it is probably better to err on the side of grace. Sometimes your children won't understand some of their own pain, and you must be graceful in helping them deal with it. At times they will lash out at you just because you are there. You don't deserve it just as they don't deserve your grace, but that is what the Gospel of Jesus Christ is all about— undeserved grace. As His followers, we are living and breathing recipients of that unmerited grace, and we are commanded to show that grace to others.

As a parent, living each step and each day one moment at a time is essential. Too often we are focused on the end result, wanting our kids to turn out perfect. We want them to be good, responsible adults, and we try to accomplish that by living in a frenzy, rushing through each day impatient to see *that* happen. In reality, when our children finally "arrive" as adults, we may be surprised, for God is able to have them end up exactly where they should be—in His will.

That is why taking each step slowly is important. Now in the grandparenting stage, I look at my children who are raising their children, and I celebrate the growth I see in them and the way they are raising our grandchildren. But sometimes I already hear them talking about when their children are going to be adults. That is when I tell them to slow down and enjoy the process. In other words, prepare for A to Z, but live from A to B. Live for the moment you are in and trust God for the future.

Throughout this entire parenting process thus far, one

important lesson I have learned is that humility is more important than humiliation. Our family has learned to be humble and lay our lives before the Lord throughout this journey. Like any parent, I had an image I wanted to keep. I wanted people to think my family walks on water and everything is great, but I have had to realize that is not true. Instead of being humiliated, my wife and I chose to be humble and to rely on the Lord to give us strength as parents and not worry about what people say.

No matter where you are in the parenting journey, other people will continually question how you handle things. But it doesn't matter what other people think; what matters is what God thinks. He is the creator of your life and your children's lives. So simply rely on Him and ask Him for the strength to live for today. Ask Him to help you prepare for A to Z but live from A to B. Seek first His kingdom and righteousness as you learn to parent with grace and truth.

ABOUT THE AUTHOR

Dan Seaborn is the founder of Winning At Home, an organization that supports marriages and families, and director of the Marriage & Family Division of AACC. As an author and speaker, Dan uses humor, practical illustrations, and real-life examples to teach others how to *win at home*. He has authored twelve books and holds a master's degree in Christian ministries.

NOTES

Chapter 3. The Truth about Discovering Your Children's Unique Talents and Abilities

1. "Family Dinner Linked to Better Grades for Teens," ABC News, September 13, 2005, http://abcnews.go.com/WNT/Health/story?id=1123055&page=1.

2. "The Importance of Family Dinners VIII," The National Center on Addiction and Substance Abuse, September 2012, www.centeronaddiction.org/addiction-research/reports/importance-of-family-dinners-2012.

3. Lawrence J. Cohen, "The Drama of the Anxious Child," Time, September 26, 2013, http://ideas.time.com/2013/09/26/the-drama-of-the-anxious-child/.

Chapter 6. The Truth about Blended Families

1. "Dad Surprises Stepdad at Daughter's Wedding—with Both Walking Bride Down Aisle," Today, September 30, 2015, http://www.today.com/parents/dad-surprises-stepdad-daughters-wedding-both-walking-bride-down-aisle-t46981.

Chapter 7. The Truth about the Roles of Mom and Dad

1. US Census Bureau, "Children's Living Arrangements and Characteristics: March 2011," table C8 (Washington, DC), cited in "Statistics on the Father Absence Crisis in America," National Fatherhood Initiative, 2016, http://www.fatherhood.org /father-absence-statistics.

2. John P. Hoffmann, "The Community Context of Family Structure and Adolescent Drug Use," Journal of Marriage and Family 64 (May 2002): 314–330, cited in "Statistics on the Father Absence Crisis in America," National Fatherhood Initiative, 2016, http://www.fatherhood.org/father-absence-statistics.

3. D. L. Lang, T. Rieckmann, R. J. DiClemente, R. A. Crosby, L. K. Brown, and G. R. Donenberg, "Multi-Level Factors Associated with Pregnancy among Urban Adolescent Women Seeking Psychological Services," Journal of Urban Health 90 (2013): 212–23.

4. A. N. Allen and C. C. Lo, "Drugs, Guns, and Disadvantaged Youths: Co-occurring Behavior and the Code of the Street," Crime & Delinquency 58, no. 6 (2012): 932–53.

5. US Census Bureau, Family Structure and Children's Living Arrangements 2012, Current Population Report, July 1, 2012.

6. Fulton County, Georgia, jail populations, Texas Department of Corrections, 1992.

7. "Absent Parent Doubles Child Suicide Risk," Sid Kirchheimer, WebMD, January 23, 2003, http://www.webmd.com/baby/news/20030123 /absent-parent-doubles-child-suicide-risk.

8. Margaret J. Meeker, Strong Fathers, Strong Daughters: 10 Secrets Every Father Should Know (Washington, DC: Regnery Publishing, Inc.) 2006), cited in "The Father and Daughter Relationship," Deep Roots at Home (blog), June 2, 2012, http://deeprootsathome .com/the-father-and-daughter-relationship/.

9. Ibid.

10. "24 Awesome Things Moms Do," Rachel Marie Martin, Finding Joy, April 2014, http://findingjoy.net /24-awesome-things-moms-do/#.V6t4i4WcHeI.

11. Timothy S. Grall, "Custodial Mothers and Fathers and Their Child Support: 2007," US Census Bureau, November 2009, http://www.census.gov /prod/2009pubs/p60-237.pdf.

SCRIPTURE INDEX

NOTES

NOTES

NOTES

NOTES

NOTES

ARE YOUR KIDS OBSESSED
WITH THEIR PHONES?

52 Ways to Connect with Your Smartphone Obsessed Kid
by Jonathan McKee
Paperback / 978-1-63409-707-9 / $12.99

In *52 Ways to Connect with Your Smartphone Obsessed Kid,* author Jonathan McKee offers just the help you need to have meaningful interaction with your kids instead of always overreacting to their unhealthy consumption of technology and media. In a world where over 80 percent of 12- to 17-year-olds now own a smartphone, parents are searching for ways to pry their kids' eyes from their devices and engage them in real, face-to-face conversation. McKee—drawing from his 20-plus years of experience working with teenagers, studying youth culture, and raising three teens of his own—provides an abundant supply of useful tips and creative ideas to help you bond with the Smartphone Generation.

Jonathan McKee is an expert on youth culture and the author of more than twenty books, including *52 Ways to Connect with Your Smartphone Obsessed Kid, More Than Just the Talk, Get Your Teenager Talking,* and *The Guy's Guide to God, Girls, and the Phone in Your Pocket.* He has over twenty years of youth-ministry experience and speaks to parents and leaders worldwide. For more from Jonathan, go to TheSource4Parents.com or follow him on Twitter.com/InJonathansHead.